Pr

Romans 5:3, 4 says, "Not only so, but we also glory in our suffering, because we know that suffering produces perseverance; perseverance, character; and character, hope...."

God's Girl chronicle's Molly story of suffering and hope, beauty and tragedy, setback and triumph, all within the beautiful tapestry of God's redemption plan in Jesus. Read Molly's story and learn to rely more desperately on the God who never forsakes His people.

Brad Holcomb Pastor at Redemption Hill Church

❧ ☙

I've had the pleasure of knowing Molly all of her life. Throughout her childhood and teen years, Molly was surrounded by a loving family, church community and group of friends. Molly was the girl in Sunday School who sat quietly and listened when you were teaching. She was the girl in youth group who studied her Bible, asked questions, memorized verses and wanted to grow in her faith.

There were the small difficulties of life for her, to be sure, but these were preparing her for the larger ones. Jeremiah 12:5 asks: "If you have raced with men on foot, and they have wearied you, how will you compete with horses? And if in a safe land you are so trusting, what will you do in the thicket of the Jordan?"

Little did she know that her early life was preparing her to 'run with horses' and that she would become familiar with the 'thicket of the Jordan.' Life often prepares us unknowingly for what is coming in the future. Remarkably, Molly started her journey the night of her wedding. Molly is unique and her story is unique. It is a testimony to God bringing beauty from the ashes and the unrelenting power of the Holy Spirit to transform us into the image of Jesus Christ. Sit quietly and listen to what God can do.

April Bowman, Pastor's wife, Molly's childhood church

I was only 13 at the time of Molly's stroke. David was my youth pastor at the time. I remember sitting in our youth room when they announced her stroke and asked us to pray. I remember feeling shocked because Molly and David were so young, and not too long before, my grandfather had passed away from a stroke.

Reading this book now, years later, Molly's story deeply impacts me and encourages me in my faith. My wife and I are currently working as church planters in southern Mexico. We're new to church planting; we just moved here about 7 months ago. We're also new to being married, only about 2 years in.

Our faith is strong, and our lives are fully surrendered and led by the Lord, but life has never been harder than now. It's hard adapting to life in Mexico, and the spiritual disciplines we had in the States don't seem to have the same effects they used to.

Reading *God's Girl*, as painful as it is, has deeply encouraged us in our faith as Molly's faith is put to the test. Time and time again, she brings her pain to the Lord, receives His comfort, and keeps her focus on loving Him and those who do not yet know Him.

Molly's faith encourages us, and brings us back to the core truths that following God does not guarantee shelter from pain and hardship, but He does promise that He will always be with us and for us. This truth is deeply evident in Molly's story.

Gabe Garcia, missionary to Mexico

❧ ☙

We've known Molly for over 20 years. From her teenage years until now, Molly's story is one of deep faith and trust in God. She understands and lives into her identity as a child of the Most High King. *Matt & Marrilee Boldt Worship Pastors, childhood church, CA*

❧ ☙

God's Girl is vulnerable and haunting, but filled with faith, hope, and love. Molly's story probably isn't your story, but her story is found in all our stories—suffering and loss, complexity and chaos, but finding that Jesus is enough.

Jim Essian, Senior Pastor at Paradox Church,
Author of Jesus For You

❧ ☙

I first met Molly in elementary school through AWANA. I was in third grade; she was in fifth. In a lot of ways, she was the older sister I never had. We use words like brother, sister, and family to describe Christian fellowship. However, Molly genuinely lives it. Molly was the one who made sure the whole group was included in the fun, who took responsibility and acted in wisdom beyond her years, who honestly took an interest in other people, who encouraged this shy, awkward dweeb to open up more.

I remember what a shock it was to everyone when Molly suffered a stroke. We were all very worried. It was a revelation to me that everyone, regardless of age or health, is susceptible to such a tragic experience. It was the first time a friend, as well as someone I knew from within my generation, had undergone a severe level of affliction. I mean, who expects to suffer a stroke and have open heart surgery when she is a healthy 20 years old? Talk about a test of faith!

Although I only saw Molly a handful of times thereafter, I never ceased praying for her and God's healing, physically, mentally, emotionally, and spiritually. We lost touch shortly after her surgery, aside from the occasional Facebook post.

It wasn't until several years later that she reached out to me. I had been living as a missionary in Germany for a year when she sent me a message to encourage me that I had been in her thoughts and prayers. Apart from immediate family, one couple, and my sending churches, Molly was the only person from the western hemisphere to ask me how I was doing. She sincerely cares about people; that is the fruit of the Spirit made evident in her. Since then, Molly has faithfully partnered with me in sharing the gospel in every way imaginable short of flying to Europe herself.

To those reading this book, I pray you find it encouraging. I certainly did. Molly is authentic and vulnerable in a way so few authors are. Hers is a story of true faith to her Redeemer when weaker souls would choose to stop following.

Zach McKay, Missionary to Germany

❧ ☙

GOD'S GIRL

A Memoir of Surrender in Suffering

GOD'S GIRL

A Memoir of Surrender in Suffering

Molly Mulano

WildSocksPress

ISBN 978-1-7349152-5-9
ISBN 13: 978-1-7349152-5-9 (Wild Socks Press)

Published by Wild Socks Press
Editor Dionne Carpenter
dionne@wildsockspress.com
Nampa, ID
www.wildsockspress.com

Molly Mulano may be reached at mollymulano@gmail.com and follow her at Facebook Molly Mulano.

Bible versions less frequently quoted in this book will be noted by the spelled-out name the first time and then noted by initials for later usages. Example: New American Standard Version NASV, then NASV.

Book Cover designed by Justin Anderson.

Dedicated

To Jesus: Thank You for carrying me through my life, because I could not even walk on my own. You enabled me to not only walk but share my story through suffering. I'm thankful You have called me Your own. You are my best friend, loving Redeemer, and faithful Savior.

To Alex: My joy in the midst of suffering. I love you.

To all who are in a season of suffering—whether it is physical, mental, emotional, or spiritual—I write this book for you.

A Note

I wrote this as a memoir by intentionality. Every part of my own story that you will read in this book is true experience faithfully reported.

For reasons that will become obvious as the story progresses, many names and identifying details have been disguised to protect from the guilty as well as to give much needed protection to the innocent.

I changed the name of the man I married to David because I prayed for him to be like David in the Old Testament—a man after God's own heart. Jesus commands me to love Him, my neighbors, and my enemies. I try to do that.

Preface

Why am I sharing my story? Is it because I am proud and want people to look at my life and say that I have done a good job? Is it because I crave attention from other people? No. I have waited thirteen years to write because I have not wanted to share with the world what I have been through.

This is not a fairytale of me getting married to the man of my dreams and living happily ever after. My story is messy. Raw. Emotional. My life has been filled with hardships and suffering. In telling my story, I also share the difficulties my extended family has had to endure.

And yet, my story is also filled with hope. I write to emphasize that God is gracious and good. He takes care of me in my hard times—providing for me time and time again. Trusting the Lord is hard, but He is worthy and glorious.

I hope and pray that as you read my story you will believe in Jesus, and know that He loves you so much that He came to earth, died on the cross for you, and rose from the dead.

TABLE OF CONTENTS

CHAPTER 1

Suffering

I was so excited to marry my best friend David after being friends for 10 years. We were married on April 17, 2010. We had a big wedding. I had just turned 20 and David was 21. After the wedding, we stayed at a hotel in La Jolla, California near the place where we used to play as kids.

That night, our first night together on our honeymoon, I was standing in the hotel room while David was in the bathroom. All of a sudden, I felt a bang on my chest, and I fell down onto the bed.

That's odd, I thought.

I dismissed it, got back up, and headed to my suitcase to get the journal I had kept for years to give to my husband. David walked out of the bathroom and looked startled. As I tried to talk, I found that my mouth wouldn't communicate. I tried to say, "What's wrong with me?" but the words came out all jumbled.

David quickly took me into the restroom to look at the mirror, and I noticed that my face had dropped on the right side.

David said, "We're going to the hospital." I shook my head no, but he insisted, so I walked with him holding me up. As we passed the pool, I tripped and stumbled.

We reached the front desk, and David talked to the staff about calling an ambulance. We had no phones at the time because we had wanted to get away for the week after the wedding. David did the talking, and I remember being frustrated that I could not form the words to speak.

When the ambulance arrived, I was carried because I still couldn't walk. I heard someone saying something to me, but I couldn't talk to them. I heard machines binging as David held my hand. I was dizzy, weak, then I went blank.

ꟹ ꟹ

What is suffering? For whom is this book written? Why are you reading this book? Are you curious about suffering? Have you suffered? Has someone close to you suffered? According to the dictionary, **Suffering is "the state of undergoing pain, distress, or hardship."** Nearly everyone has undergone suffering to some extent.

The suffering you've experienced may be brief or it may be long-term. It could be a bodily trauma like childlessness, miscarriage, cancer or a debilitating condition like blindness, heart failure or multiple sclerosis. Maybe someone you loved died of COVID.

You may have experienced some form of abuse by family members, romantic partners or bullies who call you worthless, or who play mind games on you that keep you trapped mentally. Or maybe you struggle to overcome the ravages of getting raped, trafficked or terrorized without mercy.

Maybe you are depressed, anxious, suicidal or OCD. Or maybe your tour in a war zone left you with PTSD that you can't shake off.

Your suffering might be the persecution for your faith by your extended family, your culture or an oppressive government that seems to have utter control over whether you live or die. You may feel isolated from like-minded believers. Or maybe your Christian service has left you with scars and disappointment. Maybe you've prayed for someone's salvation for years and they're still not saved.

Maybe "justice" was NOT just for you. You experience the daily unfair struggles to survive at your job and keep food on your table.

That's suffering. That's physical suffering. That's emotional suffering. That's mental suffering. That's spiritual suffering.

I weep for you. I empathize with you. I have been there, and know others who have experienced that suffering, including people in Bible times who have encouraged me in my faith.

As I prayed about which Scripture to share in this first discussion about suffering, 2 Corinthians 1:3-7 came to mind. These verses capture my heart for you if you suffer today:

> Blessed be the God and Father of our Lord Jesus Christ, the Father of mercies and God of all comfort, who comforts us in all our affliction, so that we may be able to comfort those who are in any affliction, with the comfort with which we ourselves are comforted by God. For as we share abundantly in Christ's sufferings, so through Christ we share abundantly in comfort too. If we are afflicted, it is for your comfort and salvation; and if we are comforted, it is for your comfort, which you experience when you patiently endure the same sufferings that we suffer. Our hope for you is unshaken, for we know that as you share in our sufferings, you will also share in our comfort.

I hope you will find the abundant comfort I found. That is why I share my story for all those who are suffering—whether your trials are small or heavy. I don't know your story. But God does.

I have struggled a lot with pride and self-righteousness. The Lord has humbled me and taught me that His greatness is greater than me. Jesus brings me comfort because He has suffered more than I have. He has saved me from my sins by dying on the cross and rising from the dead. I plead for you to take a look at your own heart and ask Jesus for help.

I hope and pray that you meet Jesus—He's been my best friend. Throughout my loneliness, He is with me always. I hope and pray that if you're not a Christian, that you will decide to follow after Him. Love Him. He loves you and doesn't shame you, but asks you to follow Him. And if you are a Christian, I hope and pray that you would continually recognize God's amazing love for you—even in suffering.

Another passage I'd like to share is 2 Corinthians 4:7 from The Passion Translation:[1] "We are like common clay jars that carry this glorious treasure within, so that the extraordinary overflow of power will be seen as God's, not ours."

Please realize that God is so powerful and grand. I am nothing more than a person who keeps on sinning, as you will see throughout my story. I am "common"—just an ordinary girl. I am God's girl, yes, but the key word is "God's." God has extraordinary power, and I pray that you would open your eyes and glimpse who He is.

May you be astonished at how He is the Author of your life (Hebrews 12:1-3); your Lover (Hosea 2:14, 16, 19, 20); and your Father (Romans 8:15). Please recognize Jesus as your Good Shepherd (John 10:14-18); your Strength and Shield from the storms of life (Psalm 28:7); and the One who "bore our griefs and carried our sorrow" (Isaiah 53:4). May you see the Holy Spirit as your Helper (John 14:26, 27) and Counselor (Revised Standard Version, RSV), but also as your Sanctifier (1 Peter 1:2)—to set you apart and declare you as holy.

In the next few chapters, I'm going to tell my story. I did not grow up in suffering, though some of my friends were suffering and I wept for them. When I was 20, my world turned upside down. The Lord has taken me on a journey that is hard and uncomfortable to talk about.

This is my story.

❧ ☙

[1]By the way, a friend gave me a copy of The Passion Translation during the lonely times of deepest suffering and I found it enormously comforting. The majority of the Bible verses I have included are from the ESV and NIV passages. However, the Spirit used some of The Passion Translation to speak to me. I have checked to ensure faithfulness to the ESV and NIV whenever I have included verses from the TPT.

CHAPTER 2

Growing Up

Growing up with my dad, mom, and younger sister fostered security in a comfortable living arrangement in San Diego, California. I did not live in fear of pleasing my parents because they loved me. I felt safe, secure. When I was five years old, I prayed to accept Jesus into my heart, and I really believed in Him. Several years later, when I was in the 3rd grade, I was baptized.

My mom chose to homeschool my sister and me when I was in 3rd grade because I was unable to read. It was during this time that I met David, and we became close friends. He was in 5th grade, also homeschooled by his mother.

Just before I left for 6th grade camp, David told me in confidence that his family might be moving away. I wrestled with the news all the way to camp. After I got to camp, I fainted in the First Aid class because the talk of blood was overwhelming, and I was sent to my room. I cried out of embarrassment for fainting, and because my best friend might be moving away.

I left my dorm room to get tissues and a woman stopped me. She noticed my tears and asked me what was wrong. My fear of David moving with his family spilled out of my mouth. The woman comforted me and expressed her love for Jesus. She had gotten pregnant twice before she turned eighteen, then had met Jesus and welcomed Him into her heart. She met a wonderful man and married him, but Jesus was everything to her, and she wanted me to know Christ too.

The woman told me that whether or not David would end up moving away, Jesus would always love me and be with me. I wanted to be free of my anxiety and have that kind of love for Christ. From that moment, I rededicated my life to Christ. As my mom drove me home from camp, I kept thinking about that woman's passion for Jesus.

The following year, David and his family moved away to Dallas, Texas. I cried, but Jesus' faithful love sustained me. I began a daily prayer list, and moved from reading a daily proverb to diving deeper into my Bible. I read more than thirty missionary books, including ones by Amy Carmichael, Corrie ten Boom, and Gladys Aylward.

I wanted to save the world, but instead learned to listen to Jesus and followed His lead. Being heavily involved in church included a weekly Thursday night Bible study, teaching 3rd and 4th grade Sunday school, fasting once a year for thirty hours for the children in Africa who didn't have food to eat, five house builds in Mexico, and three mission trips around the world. I went to AWANA (an after-school program that focused on Jesus, memorizing Bible verses, and studying the Bible), participated in all the AWANA scholarship camps, and was involved in all the AWANA events.

I was also involved in a teen pregnancy center for a year and led a few Bible studies of my own. My life at this time centered around doing whatever I could do for Jesus. I loved Him and wanted other people to love Him too.

The Holy Spirit led me to make these decisions, and I followed. I would often pray for direction on where to go and what to do, and eventually He would lead me with a clear Yes or No or give me a passage of Scripture as guidance.

Sometimes, I obeyed immediately. Other times, I wouldn't listen because I was proud, selfish, or didn't like His answer. I didn't like many of the Holy Spirit's answers. I felt as though I was right, and what could God know? Yet, the Holy Spirit was gentle, patient, and kind to me until I said "Yes Lord," and did it.

Many people would look at me oddly when I would tell them what the Spirit said to me. They would often say I was hearing things incorrectly—that God doesn't work that way—and that certain spiritual gifts such as hearing the Holy Spirit are dead. I struggled with pleasing people instead of pleasing God, and as a result I said Yes to doing a lot of different spiritual things—which wore me out.

I filled over twenty-five different journals and wrote all sorts of poetry at this point, including the following poem.

God's Girl

I've searched in many places,
And tried to find fulfillment there,
But my purpose isn't different faces,
Or to simply breathe fresh air.

I am not my own,
My life belongs to Christ.
I live for Him alone,
My will I sacrificed.

To God I give my heart,
All my passionate devotion.
My love for Him will never part,
I give Him my sea of emotion.

My tears are also His to keep,
As He wipes them all away,
His peaceful comfort runs so deep,
As He reminds me of His love today.

He loves me as one loves His bride,
With tenderness, He holds me,
For me He willingly did die,
And He rose again so powerfully.

By my side He shall remain,
Through joy and laughter,
Through tears and pain,
Today, yesterday, and hereafter.

Never will He abandon me,
His faithfulness will not end,
Nor His grace and majesty,
For, bravely, He will defend.

To Himself, He draws me near,
He longs for intimacy,
His gentle love He has made clear,
For He desires to be with me.

Unchanging is His perfect love,
Forever will He proclaim,
His passion from above,
His humility and His fame.

Jesus is my loving King,
I trust Him with my very life,
Of His praise I shall always sing,
He's forgiven my sinful strife.

God's my True Love and I'm His girl,
My heart stirs at His calm voice,
His touch is more soothing than any pearl,
I've fallen in love by choice.

Not even when life gets tough,
Will His amazing love ever perish.
Through the smooth and the rough,
His love and presence I truly cherish.

-MG '05

ঌ ৵

David and I managed to stay in contact over long-distance for six and a half years. When I was in eighth grade, and he was in tenth, he told me that he loved me, but we were too young to start anything. We talked via email and through letters. We saw each other about once a year. Then, when I was in eleventh grade, my family flew out to Texas.

During our visit, David gave me a white gold cross necklace and a silver jewelry box with three embedded roses on top. He told me that he loved me, wanted to spend his life with me, and asked me to go on a date with him. I eventually said yes. For the next three and a half years, David and I dated while living in separate states.

God sustained me as I waited through our years apart. I remember being frustrated with the statistic that few couples make it through long distance relationships, but I knew that the missionaries Jim and Elisabeth Elliot endured a long-distance relationship for a while. Elisabeth's book *Passion and Purity* helped me. One notable quote from the book read,

> I realized that the deepest spiritual lessons are not learned by His letting us have our way in the end, but by His making us wait, bearing with us in love and patience until we are able to honestly pray what He taught His disciples to pray: Thy will be done.

Below is one of the journal entries I penned during this time—when I was seventeen years old:

July 5, 2007

We spent a couple hours at Borders today. Like normal, I made my way to the Christian literature section. Elisabeth Elliot published Jim Elliot's journals into one thick book. His legacy draws me closer to Christ and God encouraged me through Jim's honesty.

I can relate, though only slightly, to their struggle of longing to be together while God asked them to wait. If I recall correctly, they dated for five years, and most of the time had contact through letters alone because they were in different states or countries. Then they were married for three years and had a baby girl before Jim was martyred on the shores of Ecuador.

I greatly admire their obedience to God. Jim journaled about aching to be with his Betty, yet he knew God wanted them to wait. So, they waited. David and I waited seven years from the time we became friends until two months ago when we became an official couple. Now we have a lot more waiting to do. I am thankful technology has improved so that we can talk on the phone and email often.

I admire how the Elliots sought God for help and He helped them wait for His timing. Yes, the wait was difficult and they struggled, but God was their strength. I pray God will be the strength of David and myself to help us wait. Neither we nor the Elliots could ever wait out of our strength, for we are weak.

I benefited immensely from Jim's blunt honesty about how he longed to hold Betty and to be her husband. Page after page, he journaled about how much he loved and missed her and did not understand why God still asked them to wait. Yet they waited, and then one day God gave them permission to marry and they were married. The Elliots truly loved each other and loved Christ even more.

I want to love Christ like them. I want to love as they loved, knowing the road will be bumpy and knowing God will always walk with me. In reality, I have no idea where He will lead, what will happen, or any specifics about the journey ahead.

As of now, He is guiding me to inner city ministry while attending Wheaton College in Illinois, but if He takes me someplace else then so be it.

I do love David and I long to be his wife, but if God says no, or wait, then so be it. At this moment, God says wait—trust Me and wait. I don't know what will happen in the future and neither did the Elliots. Yet, they obeyed God.

As I write, I'm sitting on a bench in my cousin's backyard in Virginia. The sky is cloudy with a variety of gray and brightness. My cousin revealed to me yesterday that I complain a lot and tend to be pessimistic. As much as I'd like to write that she is wrong, the truth is she is right. I often focus on the pouring storms of life and not pause to appreciate the beauty in the storms. The contrast between the overcast sky and the fresh, live trees is magnificent. Talk about a work of art! God is magnificent.

Yes, sin is still ugly, but I need to start noticing the goodness around me too. God uses the storms in our lives to help us realize we need to seek shelter in Him. The Lord is my refuge and my strength, as He was to the Elliots.

Lord, You do have a plan for my life and I can trust You. Forgive me, for I am a very selfish and stubborn child. I'm not delighting in You, yet expecting You to give me the desires of my heart. I know You're not Santa Claus and I realize, as a good Father, You won't give me whatever I want. You know better than I do and You alone see the whole picture. I really do want to have more faith in You. Please change my heart. Thank You so much for never giving up on me. Thank You, Jesus, for dying in my place. Thank You so much for Your love and grace.

God's girl,
Molly Grace

ᔕ ᔓ

I had to wait to be with David, and God taught me to wait patiently. Throughout the Psalms, God commanded people to wait patiently. The Lord spoke to me through such verses, but being rather impatient, I cried out to God for help.

My friends had their significant others beside them, and my David was far away in Texas. I tried to "fix my eyes on Jesus" (Hebrews 12:1, 2) and sometimes I did, but in all honesty, there were times when I didn't.

I spent a lot of time with my friends, and I listened to their struggles and stories. Some of my friends were on drugs, raped, abused, or tried to commit suicide. Some were pregnant. Many of them had come from broken homes. I wished for all of them to meet Jesus and be emotionally healed by Him. I wanted other people to find their identity in Christ. But I also wanted to help them with their emotional struggles.

I prayed for all of my friends. I also prayed about what I should do after high school. Led by my desire to help others, I decided to attend Wheaton College in Illinois.

When I moved from San Diego to Wheaton, I didn't know anyone. However, eventually I became friends with Susan, who lived next door in the dorms. I also was involved with inner city kids—serving as a Big Sister for a girl in inner city Chicago, volunteering to watch babies at a Chicago church, and spending the summer as a counselor at a camp in Kentucky.

In the meantime, David had moved back to California to be the youth pastor at my childhood church. In November 2009, he proposed and I said yes! Below is my journal entry from that wonderful day:

November 5, 2009

David and I are engaged!!!!! *Oh, thank You Father for Your grace and for giving me the gift of David!*

He completely surprised me and I'm still in shock. Apparently, David has been planning on proposing since July. So many people were included in the planning. David flew here yesterday. He had arranged with a friend from back home to Skype me when he arrived on Wheaton's campus so that I'd be in my room and not see him.

Since today is Susan's birthday, I skipped my classes so I could go out to lunch with her. We had a great time and conversation. Apparently, it was the hardest two hours of her life because I kept talking about how I was learning to trust God more but struggling about not being engaged. Susan knew David was about to propose but couldn't say anything.

She prayed for God to cloud my mind so I wouldn't figure out the plan, and God answered her prayer. While at lunch, Susan received a text from David to hurry back. She made up an excuse to get back, so we walked to the campus.

As soon as we arrived back on campus, Susan handed me a letter. I was utterly confused because the envelope said "My best friend" in David's handwriting. I read the letter from David, which was about us being best friends. A second note said to go to the chapel.

On the stage was David's Bible and a letter titled "My sister," where he explained how I'm his sister in Christ. At that point I guessed he was proposing. The note sent me to the Fireside Room and another letter in an envelope with the words "My greatest blessing."

After that, the letter told me to go to the café, and there a friend handed me a fourth letter titled "My helper." From there, I was sent to my dorm, and a letter on my bed waited for me with the words "My most important ministry."

From my room, I was told to go up to the roof. As I opened the door, I saw red roses in a vase on a table. I walked toward the roses and noticed a ring—turned around and embraced David.

He motioned for me to sit on the bench, and he bent down on his knees to propose. I can't quite remember precisely what he said, but it was something about how he would be honored to love, cherish, serve, and provide for me the rest of our lives. With a smile, David held my hands and asked if I would marry him.

With a smile so big I could burst, I responded I would be honored, and yes, I would marry him. We embraced, and he placed a beautiful, dainty, white gold, three small diamonds, perfect-for-me ring on my left ring finger. God's plans are so much better than anything we ever plan. I'm completely overcome with thankfulness.

I moved back to California after Christmas and was involved in David's church youth group while keeping up with my studies at Wheaton online. David and I finally lived in the same city for three months before we got married.

David battled depression off and on growing up. We tackled this too, trusting the Lord to help David live another day. Little did we know that it was my own life that would almost end.

CHAPTER 3

Hospital Honeymoon

I remember waking up around midnight to see my beloved David and another one of my friends in the hospital room. Apparently three days had passed. Somehow, I knew I had experienced a stroke and couldn't talk. My right hand was curved inward and rested on my chest. My right foot and leg were paralyzed too.

I remember telling David something, but I was unable to communicate with him. I felt something uneasy near my bottom side. I didn't like it. I wanted it gone. I tried to take it out with the left side of my body, but the nurses came in and told me to leave it in because I was unable to get up and go to the restroom. There were so many needles in my arm and fingers. I went back to sleep.

The next morning, I woke up to see my sister and mom in the room. They tried to cheer me up and I laughed. I said something, and my sister tried to understand what I was saying.

I wanted to know what time it was, and I pointed to the clock. My glasses were not on my face, and I couldn't read the clock. My contacts were gone, or at least I thought they were gone. *Did someone take them out? What time was it?* My sister brought me the clock and I sighed, unable to communicate. Realizing, she said, "Oh! It's 9:45 am." I sighed again, wanting to thank her but I was unable to form the words. I tried, but the noise sounded more like "Grrubmel."

I looked around and noticed there was writing on the walls, pictures of people who loved me, and notes for me to feel better soon. So many people wrote to me, and I cried and was touched by their prayers.

Why did I skip over the pages on strokes in my class at Wheaton? What was it again that I'm supposed to be having a hard time with? Where are my glasses? And contacts? Did someone take them out? I can't read the writing on the wall, so I assume someone took out my contacts.

I really wish I could read my Bible. I guess I'll recall the stuff I already remember. It's a good thing I memorized the book of Philippians at Wheaton...I guess I'll start at the beginning.

"Paul and Timothy, servants of Christ Jesus..." *Help me be Your Servant, Jesus. I feel useless, I want to do something for You. And You have me paralyzed, unable to talk to anyone other than You. Thank You, Lord, for listening to me.*

Lord, would Your Will be done even here? Please reach the nurses and the other patients? Please let someone share the gospel with them?

"...Grace to you and peace..." *Lord, please shower me with Your grace and peace? I'm a mess. Please let Your grace and peace overflow to all the people here. Please let Your grace abound.* "...making my prayer with joy..." *Lord, I do not have joy. Please help me to have joy.*

"...And it is my prayer, that your love may abound more and more, with knowledge and all discernment..." *Oh Lord, help me grow in Your love, growing more in knowledge and discernment...* "...so that you may approve what is excellent, and so be pure and blameless..." *Help me be pure and blameless...* "...filled with the fruit of righteousness that comes through Jesus Christ, to the glory and praise of God..." *Oh yes Father God! Help everything in my life praise You and bring You glory! I'm tired and I think I'm going to sleep for now...*

My neurologist was the best doctor I had ever had. He was the doctor who figured out I had the stroke, which was apparently caused by a heart tumor. After they ran MRIs, CT scans, and other tests, they found that the tumor in my heart was a third the size of my heart, so they scheduled open-heart surgery in May to remove it.

I remember one of our family friends came to the hospital. She was our wedding photographer, and she rushed her work on the photos to get them to me as soon as possible. I woke up and saw her showing the photos she had taken of the wedding to my mom and sister.

At first, I was upset that she showed them to my family before letting me see them. But then I remembered I had had a stroke, and calmed down a little. I was grateful that she processed the pictures so quickly and I could see them. They were beautiful.

A week went by, and they moved me to a different room from the ICU. At this point, I could wiggle my right foot. I was taken to another hospital for rehab. I re-learned how to sit up. I re-learned how to push my arm out. I re-learned how to move my right leg. I re-learned how to walk. It was hard. It hurt. But I kept pushing myself, and David motivated me during the moments when I felt like I was tired and didn't want to walk again, or move, or talk.

So many people prayed for me to get better—they prayed for my hand, foot, and mouth to heal...for the heart tumor to go away...for my body to be well again...and for me to keep on living.

David counted people from seventeen different countries—including Mexico, Brazil, Ecuador, and Canada—who were praying for me. I had once gone to these places as a teenager on mission trips.

I remember being in Brazil when I was fourteen, and I shared my testimony in front of five hundred people at one of the churches. I was so nervous and scared, but I talked about God's grace for me, and His grace for all of them. Oh, I was so thankful He showed me grace, compassion, and love! He was indeed showing me His grace again as I lay in the hospital. Oh, how good He was!

I remember sitting in my wheelchair, peering out to see an older man who had also suffered a stroke. He could talk, but he could not use his hand. He was so lonely, and I thanked God that I was not alone, for He is always with me.

I thanked Jesus for being my strength when I am weak. The Holy Spirit prayed for me, as He always prays for His own, and I thanked Him for groaning with me in my struggles.

I remember praying fervently that I would walk again, and write again, and speak again. I prayed for the people in my hospital. I was so thankful that the hospital did not allow any other patients to be in the room with me so my family and friends could sleep near me. They helped me get out of bed and use the restroom, because at that point I could only shout weird noises and press a button to get the nurse.

During this whole time, I couldn't say words to communicate. I couldn't take a shower or shave my legs. The nurses showered me, and it was awful when they would pour the water down my back. I didn't like it at all.

However, there was one particular nurse who cared for me so much. My aunt had done my hair when I got married, and she sprayed it like crazy to make it look beautiful. And because I didn't shower afterwards due to the stroke, my hair was in horrible knots. My mom and mother-in-law tried to brush my hair, but they couldn't untangle the knots. This nurse ended up patiently taking two or three pieces of my hair at a time and unknotting them.

She worked on my hair for hours and hours, when she was working and even when she wasn't working. Piece by piece, she individually separated each hair to make my long brown hair straight again.

At the rehab hospital, my husband told everyone that I needed to be alone, and only my family (and a very few close friends) could see me.

At the first hospital, there were hundreds of people from my family, church, AWANA, homeschool group, neighbors, and friends who wanted to stop by and wish me well. My room capacity only allowed for one to three people at a time, so people began camping outside in the hospital lobby.

They brought food and guitars. They sang, cried, talked, laughed, and prayed. So many believers prayed for me and sent me letters. I cried, thanking Jesus that so many people cared about me.

I also prayed for the people who did not have anyone come and visit them in the hospital. I remember seeing a man dressed completely in bandages. He looked like he had been in a fire. I thanked Jesus for protecting my face and body from horrible burns.

I always thought that others had it worse than me somehow. Jesus Himself was brutally beaten for me. He was nailed to a cross for me. He was pierced in the side for me. He rose from the dead for me.

I thanked Jesus with tears falling down my face that He had sacrificed so much for me. I prayed for the salvation of so many people, wanting them to know and feel the love of Christ.

I now felt the urgency to tell everyone to believe in Jesus, but I couldn't. So, I prayed. I prayed for them to hear and believe that Jesus is Lord and Savior.

During the time I was in the hospital, and throughout my recovery, several family members and close friends sent out Facebook updates. This was before iPhones, Twitter, TikTok, or Instagram.

Many people posted updates, including a friend of the family Henry, my friend Amy, my dad Tom, and my mom Becca. My church also kept a blog updated with my progress and needs.

Henry on May 1, 2010

Molly had a tougher day on Friday, but she's still smiling on Saturday. She's experiencing pain in her right side, which has hampered her important physical therapy. This pain may be caused by nerve "reconnection."

This morning Molly spelled out with her left-hand fingers three areas of prayer she would like from you:

1. That God would lessen the pain in her right side so she can continue the hard, good work of therapy.

2. For her husband David, that God's mercy and strength would continue to fall upon him.

3. That each of us would understand and believe that Jesus loves us so much, just as David and Molly have discovered. They want all to understand the wonderful truth that Jesus died on the cross to pay the punishment for our sins so we can become friends with God and enjoy living for Him forever.

God's word, the Bible, says, "God was reconciling the world to himself in Christ, not counting men's sins against them" (2 Corinthians 5:19). All of us have goofed up and sinned. All of us are alienated from God by our sin and we can't make amends, no matter how hard we try. But here's the good news, God no longer holds our sins against us when we believe and trust in His Son's life, death and resurrection for us.

Henry on May 3, 2010

At 1pm there was a meeting with your doctor, nurses, therapists and a few other people. They were all sitting around a big table and wheeled you in at the end. They went around, taking turns talking about you and your excellent progress. Then the doctor ended with the recommendation that you go home Friday or Saturday. He asked which one you preferred, and you said "Friday" loud and clear. Everyone laughed. We were all super excited and thankful.

ର ର

Throughout this time, I went to physical, occupational, and speech therapy while living in the hospital. I endured hard labor as I was able to walk with my right foot, taking a few steps a day. Later I was able to walk twenty steps, while holding the bar with my left hand.

With my occupational therapist, my right arm extended outward and upward. I could not open my right hand all the way, and had to use my left hand to pry my right hand open. Through my OT's suggestion, I had to sleep with a towel rolled up and placed in my right hand so that I didn't fall asleep with it tightened in.

I slowly re-learned how to walk, but the doctors had me stay in a wheelchair to be safe. It was difficult for me to eat food because the right side of my mouth was still drooping, so I was fed through a feeding tube for weeks.

I didn't like how I looked, so I didn't want any pictures taken of me. Growing up, my camera was everything to me–I took countless pictures of everyone, everywhere I went. However, in the hospital, the only person I allowed to take pictures of me was my dad.

I used my left arm to pick up my right cheek to form a smile on my face for his pictures. Dad took a photo of my sister and me that was posted on Facebook and was called "The Pointed Smile." Hundreds of people, from all over the world, posted a picture of themselves smiling with their hand holding up their smile and told me they too were praying for my recovery.

My speech therapist had me work on my mouth to lift it up, and it was hard. He also taught me how to pronounce the a, i, n, and j sounds again. I found it ironic that I had undergone speech therapy as a child, and again as an adult.

After two weeks, I re-learned how to say, "thank you." I could pronounce the first sound of my husband's first name, but not the ending. I couldn't say yes or no, but I shook my head up and down to communicate.

My little sister, Jane, was so sweet, and she often helped me to communicate with others by explaining what I needed. Sometimes she got it right away, but other times she didn't, and I would let her know by shaking my head.

In the hospital, I couldn't sleep well. I was awakened constantly by the nurses coming in to check on me, by the doctors trying to figure out what was wrong with me, and by all the machines binging and the needles in my skin.

The Lord sure taught me patience, patience, and more patience. As I was re-learning how to talk, walk, and move my right arm, I was very impatient. Yet I learned to be patient as I worked hard to regain movement.

I remember being so thankful to be alive. Jesus wanted me breathing in and out, and I thanked Him for my lungs working. I thanked Him that my heart didn't stop beating and prayed that my heart would be fixed at the surgery.

I didn't realize that people who have strokes usually do not need to have open-heart surgery. I just assumed that they did because I did. I also didn't realize how rare it was for someone my age to have a stroke.

I didn't realize that people don't have robotic open-heart surgery to remove a tumor that was 1/3 the size of my heart. I just assumed it was normal, because in my mind it was normal. The Lord protected my mind, answering prayers that He would. The Lord was kind, gracious, and merciful. Masterfully and graciously, He was working behind the scenes, just like He is today.

Looking back, I realized the stroke was God's way of warning us about the benign tumor in my heart. If the tumor had gone unnoticed, the doctors said my heart would have stopped in about three to six months, and my story would have been a very different one.

Chapter 4

Open-Heart Surgery

When I was seventeen, my camp counselor told me that my life would be harder than I imagined. Boy, was she right! I remember she talked about perseverance and hope. I had to keep going. I had to move my leg. I had to persevere. I had to look to Jesus for hope.

Thankfully, I was released from the hospital, and I was able to go to church with David before my heart surgery. I couldn't talk, my smile was halfway there, and I was in a wheelchair.

At church, we sang David Crowder Band's song "How He Loves" and I remembered how that was the last song I sang with my voice before I was married and had my stroke.

After I walked up the aisle at my wedding, I had requested our worship pastor to lead everyone in singing "How He Loves." We all sang the song, and I meant every word. The Lord led the same worship pastor to sing it again on that Sunday.

I sat in my wheelchair, hearing the words but unable to speak them. A tear dripped down my cheek, and I was torn because I could no longer communicate the words out loud. But then I remembered that God could still hear me even when no one else could. I sang the song in my heart. I cried. I accepted that He loved me so much. My stroke and my heart surgery were mere afflictions, but He loved me so much.

Facebook post on May 15, 2010

Good news is that the cardiologist and surgeon decided they didn't want to risk doing the invasive angiogram this Wednesday, May 19. Instead, they scheduled Molly to have a CAT SCAN angiogram yesterday.

This is good news on two accounts: Molly avoids the risky invasive angiogram, and she doesn't have to check into the hospital for her open-heart surgery until Thursday morning, May 20, an hour or so before her surgery.

Amy's update on May 19, 2010

Tomorrow is the big day.

They'll surgically remove the root problem...the tumor on the inside of Molly Mulano's heart.

Procedure starts at about 6:45a.m. (Pacific time) and lasts 7 hours.

The most proven-skillful hands will be at work on her at Scripps in La Jolla. Still, she has a few normal jitterbugs inside her. The amazing thing is that as her physical heart undergoes this trauma and surgery, her spiritual heart is resting on the all-sufficient grace of God. As unhealthy as her physical heart may be, her spiritual heart beats truer than it ever has.

Specific Prayer Requests are as follows:

- Surgery Safety.
- Complete and Speedy Healing.
- That the gospel would be uplifted continually through this process.
- Peace for the immediate family—David and his family, as well as Molly's family: Tom, Becca & Jane.

PRAISE! God has over abundantly provided for their medical bills and premiums throughout the next year, allowing David to be at home with Molly and continue serving his 30 hours at [the church].

How good is our God and how great is His name!!

Thank you to everyone who is praying unceasingly.

Love to you all,

Amy

On the night of May 19th, David graciously helped me prepare for my heart surgery by showering me with chemicals. The following morning, I sang, "The hills are alive with the sound of music!" Or rather, I tried to sing—I got the tune right, but my words were jumbled. I looked forward to sleeping when I would be put under. The nurses prepared me for surgery. Robotic hands opened my chest, removed the tumor, fixed the tear in my heart, and sewed me back together.

I woke up groggy and in a lot of pain. I saw my great uncle checking the machines, but I fell asleep again and woke up to David.

I remember sleeping with my glasses on because I wanted to be able to see during the time I was in the hospital. I hadn't had my Bible during my first stay in the hospital, so I treasured it the morning after my surgery, along with the ten prayer blankets, given by churches from all over the country.

Amy wrote this post on May 20, 2010

Molly is miraculously out of surgery, hours before expected. The valve was not involved at all, her heart wall and the hole in her heart was completely repaired and the tumor removed! She's beating strong. Resting well though not awake. Home stretch! Thank you, Jesus!

Molly's surgery finished about 1:15pm. Her heart started back up just fine. They were able to remove all of the tumor and repair the hole in her heart. The mitral valve had not been damaged and it looks good. The pathology report came back with good results. She is headed to ICU and they are rejoicing. The family thanks you for all your prayers.

"This is the day the Lord has made; we will rejoice and be glad in it!" Psalm 118:24

Events of May 22-26, 2010

Exhausted from the long surgery, I remember waking up on my second day at the hospital. Oh, my chest hurt so much! It felt like a brick building had fallen on me. The doctors had placed a huge amount of wadded gauze on my chest. Apparently, they had to crack my ribs open in order to do the robotic open-heart surgery. I had no idea that it would hurt as much as it did. Even with medicine, the pain was unbelievable. I remember crying out to God to please take the pain away.

A day later, my lungs were clogged and one collapsed. I had this thing that I blew into to try and "unclog" my lung, but it didn't help. People were immediately called/Facebooked/messaged to pray for the Lord to heal my lung.

I remember praying earlier, thanking God that my lungs were fine and now they weren't. I begged the Lord to heal my broken body. The doctor plugged my backside with a huge needle, and drained the water out of my lung. It was this moment that is forever scarred in my mind as the worst pain I've had to endure.

I remember thanking Jesus that He endured so much worse pain by dying on the cross for me. I could not imagine, having experienced this amount of intense pain, that someone would willingly sacrifice His life for mine.

For twenty-four hours, my lung was set to drain with the tube in my back chest. For twenty-four hours I cried, I sobbed, and I tried to be distracted. I got to pick who I wanted to visit me, and my friends came and talked about their lives.

I had lots of doctors' appointments even after my surgery. While we were waiting on one, I saw a pain chart on the wall that explained rating pain by using numbers. I was a little mad that they didn't have that sign at Scripps after my open-heart surgery. When the nurses would ask me to rate my pain, I would guess between 3-5, but according to the chart, I should have said it was more like a 7-8; probably a 10 when the chest tube was in to inflate and drain my lung.

Events on May 27, 2010

I took one last test, an echocardiogram, but I passed and got to go home. After the surgery, my occupational therapist talked to me about what progress I would like to see, and I motioned with my left hand writing. She looked surprised but wrote it down.

I missed journaling. I had hand-written over twenty-five journals in nine years. After my stroke, my mother realized I could no longer write, so she wrote in my journal and had a couple dozen of my close family and friends write as well.

For example, my Mom wrote this

I knew that David had given you a cross necklace when he first asked you to be in a relationship with him when you were seventeen. You wore that necklace every day.

The first morning in the hospital after your night in the Emergency Room, David told us that he had the chain necklace but not your cross. I prayed that you would be at peace losing it because it meant so much to you.

A few days later I was talking to Daddy about giving David money to buy you a different cross necklace. He said that one of the guys found it on the floor of your hospital room after they wheeled your bed and you out for a test.

So, the cross made it from the ER, up to the 8th floor and then back to you on Mother's Day. God was gracious yet again!

Mom wrote this on April 24 & 25, 2010

All the nurses and therapists congratulated you when they took out the feeding tube. Daddy joined you for your first breakfast...oatmeal, yogurt, & banana. You were still hungry so they brought you another full plate. You ate that too and the applesauce with your medicine.

You've been walking with the cane each day. Stepping up and down on a step. Moving balls from one basket to another. Each day you get stronger and move your right side more. God has been so gracious and we thank Him with all our hearts.

Just heard that on Thursday you walked without a cane! You said it was hard, but your physical therapist was proud.

David's Aunt Betty sent an amazing cookie basket. Dad and you had a taste in the morning. Then that evening, Mama walked into the room and saw you over in a corner.

When she got closer, she saw that you were eating cookies. Sneaking cookies! She called Daddy and David who came in and we all laughed and ate cookies with you. Now all the therapists say you can have the cookies anytime. You always were a "cookie monster" since you loved cookies.

Mom wrote this on May 27, 2010

They had to drain fluid from your lungs and it was very painful, especially at first. It was the most pain you had ever felt. And the pain lasted for twenty-four hours. They stuck a huge tube in your back to extract the fluid from your lungs. A friend of yours talked to you about her wedding to distract you. She still wanted you in her wedding, even if it meant you were in a wheelchair. It meant so much to you that she still wanted you in her wedding.

My sister wrote this letter

My Dearest Molly,

Have I told you that I love you lately? Because I do more than you'll ever believe. A funny story that Mom didn't put in is that David and I were trying to cheer you up so we took out fans and did the "Sisters" song and dance from *White Christmas.* You smiled and looked at us like we were crazy.

I'm thankful that you and David have had at least ten years as best friends before this and that he knows you so incredibly well. I know you so well too — we've always been close.

I always tried to make you laugh in the hospital. I just wanted to be right next to you every second of every day. Saying bye and going home was always the hardest thing I ever did.

But I got out a couple of times. A friend walked around with me. We'd go exploring around the hospital inside and out. It was so comforting because you weren't there to tell me to go home and sleep. Or just calm me down and listen. David and I also sat in your room while you were asleep and talked for a long time. It helped me process through everything.

You were so determined to get better, Molly. Every chance you had you'd try to get up. David would explain to you that you needed to lie down and rest. Then, right when he left, you'd try and get up again. Haha. Especially when it was just me.

When you were in the hospital, I wanted to take care of you like I knew you would me. You mean more to me than anyone else in this world. How many sisters do you think I have? I love you so much, Molly. Thank you for always being there for me and teaching me what it means to be a strong woman—not just through your studies but with your life.

You were so gracious and patient with everyone in the hospital and rehab. I know you had your moments, but I was still so inspired by you, and proud of you. I haven't forgotten how at peace and relieved you were when you got your Bible for the first time in the rehab hospital. You grabbed it out of my hands and just held on to it so dearly. The only time you kicked us out of the room was to spend time reading it.

The most amazing nurse you had was your very first nurse. He was your nurse on the 5th floor at Zion when we didn't even know it was a stroke yet because you were moving too much for them to do the MRI.

Mary, your night nurse when you were at the ICU at Zion—she was hilarious. We were always hoping that she would have you for the night shift. She'd always try to be your nurse and would come check on you even when you weren't her patient. She and David had some good, long conversations.

And then that other really amazing nurse was Chris from rehab, but you remember him. You always had the most loving and encouraging people to take care of you.

I was reading through my journal from when you were at Zion and I was thinking about how thankful I was for your facial expressions and personality—even your spunk and stubbornness. Haha. Especially your breathtaking smile.

I'm so proud of you, Molly. I really am. You and David really did live out what everyone talked about at your wedding. You lived it for the world to see.

I know that this journey is not over, even though some people think it is. I love you Molly, more than you'll ever know.

Love,

Your Jane

Another entry from my mom:

One day, your occupational therapist came to your apartment to see how she could help you with everyday life. When she encouraged you to hold the sponge with your right hand to wash dishes, she had a proud look on her face.

Mama asked her if most stroke patients are able to do that after only two months and she said, "No, they can't." You stopped, turned around to her and asked "Really?" It was encouraging.

She also encouraged you to stop using some of the handicap restroom stuff you had been using. She showed you how to carry the laundry up and down the stairs so you could start doing your own laundry.

Chapter 5

God is Good?

Now, here's the question I ask myself after thirteen years of struggling with the aftermath of my stroke: Is God good? The short answer is yes. The long answer follows below.

I was a sinner before I had the stroke and I still sin thirteen years later. We all do. We argue, want our way instead of other people's ways, we curse, we fear, we mess up, and we sin. We change our thinking, our views, our stands, our politics, our beliefs, and our bodies. We think we're right, when in fact we're wrong.

If you're anything like me, we aim for perfection, thinking that we "just barely" miss the mark…but that's just pride. In the Bible, Romans 3:23 says we all sin. Romans 6:23 says "the wages of sin is death." That means we all will one day die. The payment we owe God is perfection. Not a single sin can be in His presence.

When we're babies, we sin. When we're kids, we sin. When we're teenagers, we sin. When we're adults, we sin. When we're older adults, we sin. When we are on our deathbeds, we sin. But Jesus did not sin. He is perfect. He is God—three in one—Father, Son, and Holy Spirit. I know that is confusing but I have faith in that God.

If you continue to read Romans 6:23, the verse portrays the best news: "The wages of sin is death, but the gift of God is eternal life through Christ Jesus our Lord." God gives us this precious gift of living forever with Him. Jesus paid God the death we owed. He didn't need to die. He could have lived. He could have sent angels down to destroy the Romans. He could have used His power and might to conquer death on the cross. But He didn't stop. He bled. He suffered. He died. And three days later He rose from the dead. He's alive today in heaven!

I'm so thankful that He rose from the dead, because He conquered death. He conquered sin. He conquered life.

God doesn't change. He's perfect. He was good before I had my stroke and He still is good. Despite all the bad that has happened to me, He still is good. He is faithful, kind, compassionate, merciful, gracious, and loving. He created everything.

Yes, I don't want anyone else to go through what I did. And if they do, I'm so sorry for them. I still am a sinner. I complain. I get frustrated. I worry. But the Lord sure has taught me so much through my suffering. I treasure Jesus more because of my suffering.

A couple of weeks after my surgery, I sent out the following to all of my friends and family:

June 5, 2010

Hello everyone,

Well, here I am, seven weeks later to show that God is gracious, sovereign, and good. On the night I got married, I had a stroke. There was a tumor in my heart that broke off into my left carotid artery, thus causing the stroke. Two weeks ago, I had heart surgery to remove the tumor. Today I have problems with my right side of the body not working the way it did before April 17. Through rehab, I can walk, smile nearly all the way, and slowly type with both hands. Yet, my recovery is not identical to earlier on April 17. My body still is sore due to heart surgery, sometimes in pain. My right side stopped working and is trying to work again.

When I was in the hospital, I remember thanking God for His grace. More churches than I can count in at least seventeen different countries prayed for me. That blew my mind away. God heard every prayer and answered them by graciously sparing me and placing me here.

He sovereignly planned the timing of my stroke to happen after I was married to David, which has been a huge blessing. God is still good. In my suffering, I remember saying and believing in His goodness. Why? Because He sent His Son Jesus to die on the cross and rise from the dead for us. The suffering I went through is only a fraction of what Jesus endured for our sin, and yet He is good.

What Jesus endured was not just for me. He suffered for you too, if you believe as well. I believe Jesus redeemed me, and I look forward to the day that I can join Paul and say "To live is Christ, to die is gain."

God's girl,
Molly

Notes on life after the stroke and heart surgery

Thankfully, my insurance didn't run out after I had the stroke. When we got married, my insurance technically would have run out at the end of the month, and because of all of the doctors and the surgery, the cost would have been over two million dollars. A wealthy friend from my church had previously worked for Kaiser and talked to some people about extending my care for another year. In the end, God worked out everything! He provided in so many ways we could not see at the time. He provided for all of the hospital bills, through my parents, friends, family, and my husband.

For our (delayed) honeymoon, David surprised me by taking me to the Hotel del Coronado—one night away from everyone and everything. The view of the beach from the hotel room was incredible. David said he had sold something online to pay for it.

During my recovery, I prayed about my college education. My mom talked to Wheaton about letting me finish my classes. The college allowed me to wait and return next semester. That gives me six months to recover from my stroke.

June 22, 2010

This morning I'm at recovery for my stroke and it is journaling time. I am recovering slowly and my right side is working again. When I first had the stroke, I couldn't speak or move my entire right side. Now I'm walking without a wheelchair or walker. I'm writing with my right hand, which is stiff and sore. My speech is slowly being understood. I thank God for all of my recovery.

People from over seventeen countries and over ninety-five churches have been praying for me since I had the stroke. God hears all their prayers. I love how He is faithful and gracious. He never changes. Jesus is the same yesterday, today, and forever.

God's girl,

Molly Grace Mulano

June 29, 2010

As I write, David and I are at camp with the youth group. Right now they're on a hike and I'm at the campsite.

Lately, I've been wondering if I'm pregnant. I have thrown up often in the past few days, and I never used to throw up. Then, over the last month I have been noticing babies and smiling at them, which is odd because I never used to do that.

Honestly, I don't know if I want to be pregnant right now. David and I just talked about the possibility of me being pregnant and he has a really good heart. He didn't marry me until he felt he could be a father. I only wish we could have our full honeymoon before being parents.

I love being married to David. I love, love, love David so much. We are closer now than we were before the stroke and open-heart surgery. I remember praising God while holding David's hand the day the doctors removed the tumor.

God's girl,

Molly Grace Mulano

July 22, 2010

Well today God answered a plea of my heart. Last night I could not go to youth group, so Jane came over. We talked for a while, and I realized a few things:

1. God is good. He gives what is good.
2. God is good to me. He gave me the stroke, heart surgery, and pregnancy (Surprise!). All is a good gift from Christ. He knows I can handle it because He is my strength.
3. I lack female Christian fellowship and I'm sad.

Jane made me promise her I would call girls and I did. A few girls came over to my house and we talked about God. For the first time since I had the stroke, I invited females who love Jesus over to my house. God is good.

God's girl,
Molly Mulano

❧ ☙

My grandmother says I should abort because it's crazy for me to be pregnant right now. I immediately told her No. But in my head, I wrestled with the thought of abortion. Jesus says, "NO" so I submit. *A child is inside of me, Lord?! How am I going to parent?! How can I do parenthood?!?! Please help me!*

Also, I'm not going back to college to finish my degree. I have a child that I'm going to have to look after. My mom called the school and they gave me my classes/credits. I'm so thankful I got to go to Wheaton and learn from them. My professors and college classmates are so great, but it is not time for me to finish.

God's girl,
Molly Mulano

❧ ☙

My old college roommate came out to stay with us. Another friend from Wheaton, Susan, came over to see me. I was thrilled that she flew out from Chicago. I talked to Susan about my baby. I asked her to pray for his/her salvation. I prayed every day for Jesus to redeem this child.

I spent the summer going to rehab for the right side of my body. I didn't anticipate this at all when I first got married. I expected to get a job, have the youth group girls spend the night at my place, and have a romantic time with my brand-new husband. But no, here I was, a 20-year-old girl in occupational, physical, and speech rehab. From 9am to 3pm I went to classes to move my hand again, to walk, and to say letters. All summer.

I spent the time learning how to talk again with Mrs. Pierce. She was a speech therapist who came to my house once, twice, and sometimes three times a week, but didn't charge us. She had me read bedtime stories to my little one over and over again. She had me talk, work on my tone of voice, and pick up the speed. I was so thankful to her. I'm speaking clearly now because God used her.

During the first few months of my pregnancy, I had horrible morning sickness. I threw up every single day, some days three times a day. I could not keep meat down or cook meat because it made me throw up. I couldn't keep any food down through September, so the doctors gave me medication that helped alleviate my morning sickness most of the time. I craved bean and cheese burritos often, and thankfully David bought them for me.

In August 2010, I almost lost my baby. I bled out in the restroom at physical therapy, blood flowing everywhere for two hours straight. I had horrible cramps, and everything hurt so badly. I thought I had lost this precious child. I went in and told my PT nurse that I needed to go to the hospital because I thought my baby was gone.

Tears flowing down my face, I waited, praying for Jesus to save this child that I had come to love so dearly. David raced in and took me to the emergency room. They rushed me in. While sitting alone with David, I told him to let me die if it was necessary to save the baby. He cried and said okay. We sat in the sonogram room and grieved. Then, they ran the sonogram and we saw our baby moving. Apparently, the blood clot was below the baby, and the baby was still alive. We were so relieved!

In October we went on a house build in Tijuana, Mexico with my church. I had been on five other house builds all over Mexico when I was in junior high and high school. We were able to bless a family with a home.

Toward the end of October, I was in a Bible study, when suddenly I was in immense pain. I didn't want to interrupt the study, so I went into the restroom and cried. *What's going on? Why does it hurt so much?* One of the women came to me and asked if I was all right because she had noticed my tears. She rushed me over to David at the church, and he took me to the hospital. I was nineteen weeks pregnant and the nurse said I was two centimeters dilated. The baby wanted to come out. *It hurts so much! Is the baby going to be all right?* Tears were flowing down my cheeks as I cried out to the Lord.

The doctor did something to keep the baby inside of me. The baby was all right. *Praise Jesus!* I had to stay in so the doctor could run more tests on me. Another week in the hospital. We thought about names as we bought food (the food was given to us as a gift by a man in church).

We found out that we were having a boy, and told everyone, but waited to announce his name. We decided to call him Alex. I had anticipated it was going to be a boy, and I was so excited to meet him!

I went to so many doctors I couldn't even count them all. The hospital had me see many baby doctors, and they finally found one whose daughter had also had a stroke. The doctor was very kind, and quite a bit older than me. He gave me Vicodin when I had been in so much pain in October. He thought my driving alone to see him for my appointments was very brave. I honestly just drove alone because David was too tired to take me. David was working two jobs trying to pay the bills, and I was so grateful for David and everything he had been through for me.

In January 2011, I was sitting while David talked to our youth group. All of a sudden, I couldn't see out of my right eye. *That's odd.* I brushed it off, but when David was done and I tried to get up, I felt dizzy. I decided to take the elevator downstairs to sit in our car. Everyone was coming over later that day for my baby shower, and I was excited. *But what's going on with my sight? Oh! I can see out of my right eye again, that's good! Should I tell David? Oh, I don't know!*

Later that day we were at my parents' house waiting for my baby shower to start and I mentioned to David that my right eye didn't work while he was preaching. David was stunned and immediately called the doctors to ask for advice. We raced to the emergency room per their direction. *What's the big deal? My eyesight just went out for like 10 minutes! I'm going to miss my own baby shower!*

Doctor after doctor and nurse after nurse looked me over and ran tests. I had another MRI, but it was so loud and I could feel Alex move very fast. He did not like the sound. *Oh, please stop! My baby doesn't like it! What is going on with me, Lord? Please help the doctors find out soon!*

A week went by, and the doctors told us that I had a transient ischemic attack (TIA), a mini stroke. They gave me a lot of medication, and I was put on bed rest. The doctors also had me routinely take a needle and poke it into my leg, pumping me up with blood thinner. *Me? Using a needle on my own leg twice a day?! I have come a long way since fainting from the sight of blood at camp...*

My mom threw me another baby shower the next week, and so many thoughts flew around in my mind. *Oh man, I'm going to have a baby! Diapers. Pooping. I don't even know what it's like to have a child. And*

I'm going to be responsible for him. I'm not ready, Lord. What if I'm not good enough at being a mom for him? Lord, please save my baby. Wrap him up in Your arms. Please help me to love him, to adore him, to wrap my arms around him.

During the months leading up to Alex's birth, I just sat on the couch and read or watched a lot of television. For the full nine months of my pregnancy, I struggled with various symptoms including major heartburn, nausea, constant vomiting, and intense lower abdominal pain. The latter lasted from October to March.

My mom and I were walking at Target when labor began. I could feel it. The contractions started. And again. And again. My mom drove me home to David and, once the contractions got closer, David and I drove to that ever-familiar hospital.

There were so many doctors and nurses in my room. A nurse had to hold up my right leg because I couldn't do it on my own. Three hours of pushing and pushing. *Oh Lord, I can't do it! I'm tired, please help me get him out of my body!* The doctors said they could get a cone to help get my son out, but it might make his head narrow. I cried out "YES! Just do it!"

Sixteen hours after the contractions started, our son was born Alex Mulano. I was so nervous. *I'm only twenty-one and I have a child! What am I going to do? I don't know how to raise a child? Oh, I'm so scared, Lord! Help me raise this baby to glorify You!* The nurse walks in on me crying while holding Alex. She told me that she had heart surgery too, and that this baby is a gift. I realized the truth in her statement and thanked God for giving Alex to me.

One week later I was still in the hospital. Alex was fine, but my test results needed to come back before I would be released. I was thankful to be given my own room. The nurses and doctors wrote me a card, which was sweet of them.

Once I had returned home with Alex, I marveled at how cute he was, and at how much he cried. Two weeks later, I was back in ER for a day for gross issues with my body. The Lord was not done teaching me about Himself yet.

Two months after he was born, I reached the end of my rope, and was utterly exhausted. David suggested I drink coffee to keep me up, and although it took a while, coffee began to grow on me, especially sugary coffee drinks. Our little family ended up moving in with my parents because we needed financial help. Through the help of many people, God had provided enough money for us to live the first ten months on our own.

For our first anniversary, David and I went to a hotel in the mountains and left Alex with my parents for the night. David accidentally went through a stop sign, and the police caught us. We didn't have the registration in the car, and it was a mess. We had to pay the police so much money. We decided then and there that we're not mountain people. We're city people.

In October 2011, I decided to try and raise money by selling some of my art and photographs. My parents hosted an event, and countless people came and bought my art as well as my photography cards. I made over a thousand dollars, and it was a huge surprise.

I remember going to the bank to deposit the cash, and outside the door of the bank was a woman who was holding her baby. She begged me for money to buy her child diapers, and I pulled out a $20 bill and gave it to her. She sheepishly said, "Thank you," and walked into the nearby grocery store. I prayed for her. I understood how it felt to need money.

David flew to Chicago to meet with pastors who were starting up a new church from scratch, also known as church planting. We were interested in planting a church in San Diego that would multiply into more churches. To prepare for this, God moved us to Chicago.

CHAPTER 6

Church Planting?

After I had the stroke, we sold everything and moved to Chicago to study church planting with my former youth pastors, Josh and Samantha. They decorated one of their bedrooms with pictures of me, David, and Alex. They also found us a crib, stroller, baby toys, and diapers. A friend who lived in the same apartment building bought us baby food. We were really humbled and blessed.

Living with Josh and Samantha taught me how to live off practically nothing. I drove to Walmart and Aldi to buy the cheapest foods. We cooked together and shared not only their apartment, but every aspect of their lives. David looked for a job and applied to countless companies. He wanted to earn the money for a church plant himself rather than raise funds through support letters. However, everyone turned him down.

We went to Josh's church, but also went to Chicago to visit a church plant. There were about twenty people at the church plant, including the husband-and-wife pastors, Liam and Edith. I was so excited to meet them. David said they shared the gospel and that is what really mattered, so I agreed that we would pursue learning how to church plant from them.

Before long, David got a part-time job with a coffee shop in Chicago. In February 2012, Josh, Samantha, David, little Alex, and I packed our entire apartment and moved. We had neighbors right above us and next to us, and I had to put headphones on at nights because of the noise.

Previously, we had to use coins to wash and dry our laundry. We found a cheap washing machine in the basement. Unfortunately, the dryer didn't exactly work, and sometimes I had to dry the clothes two or three times. Sometimes the washer wouldn't work either.

Samantha taught me how to wash my clothes in the bathtub. We had an amazing tub.

The apartment was really big with five bedrooms and one enormous living room. We shared everything, just like the apostles in Acts 2. At that time, David hoped to make more money, but we didn't. Thankfully, we survived by the generosity of Josh and Samantha. Since I was not working, I had a lot of fun planning dinners for the five of us.

Edith and I had young children and started an internet playdate group to meet other moms in the area with children. I walked Alex in his stroller and met many other stroller moms. We had playdates at the park, walk dates with our strollers, and Bible studies at our houses. I met so many incredible women, and had countless opportunities to share my story and Jesus with them.

Every other week I joined Liam and several others to "chalk the block." In chalk, we would write various messages on the sidewalks such as: "Today is a gift," "Maybe the thing you're holding on to is holding you back," "Life in this place is not complete without you," "You are loved," "Love is stronger than fear," "You are beautiful," "Today miracles are waiting to happen," "Change is possible," "What you do matters," etc.

It was really good for me to use my right hand to write, and it was also a way I could give back to the city. We wrote on the streets leading up to the 'L' train, bus stops, and busy areas. We wanted people everywhere to know that they mattered. We had many people thank us for writing, and we'd invite them to our church.

One lady and I became friends because of what we wrote. She came to the church, met at my house for Bible studies, and shared her story. She told me that she had just come out of an abusive relationship and had been contemplating suicide. Then she read the "You are loved" and "Change is possible" chalk messages. She found hope and looked us up. I talked to her about Jesus. She ended up moving away, but I prayed that she would continue to find Jesus' love for her.

In August, I took my school books to Wheaton and sold them to help feed us. At that time, we hardly made any money. I remember watching the students pass by, completely unaware of what their lives in the future would look like. I prayed for them. I prayed that they would always love Jesus no matter what happened to them.

Later that year, David bought me an online journal that I could type on using my phone. This was the sweetest gift as I missed journaling so much, and my thoughts flowed faster than my physical hand could write. Below are select entries written throughout 2012-2013, with some of the names changed for privacy purposes:

December 27, 2012

Hello there, Alex is sleeping now and I figured I would journal. I'm babysitting a friend's 10-month-old little girl and she is sleeping right now too. I texted David a picture of her playing and she was so cute, calm, darling and a ham. David responded to my text asking me if she makes me want to have a girl. I replied, "No... well...no."

David doesn't want to have any more kids, and so I submit to that, but my heart is really torn. I want to raise more children, and for Alex to have a sibling. Yet, I don't want to carry another one in my belly, or have to raise the child before the age of two or three, or be really tired at all times, or go through what I endured when I was pregnant with Alex, or have to change diapers, or lots of things.

I basically want Alex to have a sibling to play with, but I don't really want to deal with any part of having another child. So, I guess I'm comfortable with not having any more children. I would totally be fine with adopting, but David doesn't think we'll be able to, given our financial situation. Well, God's in control and whatever He wants is fine by me. Jesus doesn't consider having a family as the ultimate goal in life, and I don't consider it either. "To live is Christ, to die is gain." Philippians 1:21

God's girl,
Molly

January 3, 2013

Dear Father God, I praise You for You are good, sovereign, gracious, and glorious. Thank You for ordaining everything and yet being gracious, patient enough to hear me, listen to me, and answer me while I pray. Thank you for giving David to me as my husband, as my best friend the past 14 years, and as my partner in Your ministry. Oh Lord, I'm sooo excited right now about San Diego. It looks like David, Alex, and I are moving out there sooner than I thought.

Oh, Redeemer and Provider, please let us rent the downtown apartment. Please provide David with the right job and/or support to live in San Diego.

That apartment complex seems perfect because it's for people who make less than average income...which we are currently at. And yet it's above Section 8 government housing.

Please give us furniture, beds, a table, and chairs so that we can open up a church starting in our home. Thank You Lord for Josh and Samantha and that they have opened up their home with generosity. Please bless them and take away their debt. Jesus, may Your name be known in San Diego. May You be glorious, as You always are. In Jesus' name I pray, amen.

God's girl,
Molly

January 8, 2013

I had an amazing time last night with David. Yesterday was awful, as far as Alex and I go. Samantha helped me out a little by taking him to the store, but he must have hit me, screamed, and complained all day. I did laundry yesterday too. David and I have a blocked time Monday night to talk about San Diego/theology and other heavy stuff. But I had a stress headache worrying about San Diego and about our financial situation now.

David had me talk to him about everything and he eased my discomfort, reminding me to trust our Father who took care of us before. He sent me to bed at 8pm in a quiet, dark room. I felt much better when I woke up and he came in at 2am. Then we just chatted, I cooked for us, and we cuddled. We laughed so hard and I really had a lot of fun. Then we went to sleep.

God's girl,
Molly

January 17, 2013

We're moving back to San Diego to plant a church in March 2014. I'm really happy we're following God toward that direction. Quite content. Yet, I have no clue what God has planned for us. Are our finances going to be stable? Are we going to enter persecution? Is the church just going to take off and grow? I don't know, but Jesus knows and for that I'm thankful. We're in His loving, caring, gracious hands and I trust Him.

This poem expresses my heart cry to God today.

God's girl,
Molly

Please

I'm anxious, Lord, help me,
I'm trying to please men,
All that I can be,
All that I am.

Lord, please help me,
Help me not to worry.
Help me to be
All I am at peace.

Help me to let go,
And the house be unclean,
And bending low,
Help me to intercede.

I give to You,
All that I am,
All that I see and do,
All that I have.

Thank You, Lord, for
This is all I've got,
I surrender to You more,
Please help me now.

-MGM '13

January 24, 2013

God is so amazing! David talked to the Pastor in San Diego last night and he basically offered to pay David to be on staff with his church for 6 months before they send us to go plant a church in San Diego. They are flying David out there in February and then we're all coming out there in July to stay with their church and get to know everyone. David will be their community group guy who they will send out. God is so amazing because they were praying for someone to come plant a church in that location. They already have a guy who is planting a different church in January 2014 who has the job that David is filling so it's totally God's timing for us. Praise Jesus!!

God's girl,

Molly

February 16, 2013

Today someone stayed home with Alex and I'm out of the house. I was taking pictures but then I spilled a bunch of tea on my leg. So, I'm inside Starbucks now, trying to warm up...trying.

David is in San Diego now talking, meeting, and praying with the people there. I'm so happy for him because God seems to be leading David there. Without college, without seminary, David followed God to San Diego from a big paying job in Texas to a below poverty job youth pastoring.

Then we moved to Chicago in order to follow Christ as He led David to learn pastoring from a few pastors there. David got a job that paid us very little, but that job just let David go. I'm tempted to be anxious about David's job situation, but I have to let go and trust God. He did provide for us through my stroke/heart surgery. He provided for us through my parents paying our big medical bills. He has provided for us when we moved here through Josh and Samantha's generous hearts. And provided a laptop for David from our tax return.

Philippians 4:5, 6: "The Lord is at hand; do not be anxious about anything, but in everything by prayer and supplication with thanksgiving let your requests be made known to God." I read that this morning and today I've been thinking and praying about it.

Reading down to verse 19 gives me so much hope. "And my God will supply every need of yours according to his riches in glory in Christ Jesus."

Oh Lord, I thank you for your promises, that You are rich—everything in this world belongs to You. Lord, we are poor. We need You to supply for our needs by providing a job for David. Help us to rely on You for our finances. Help us both to trust You with our hopes, dreams, and plans. Father God, I pray that we'll be able to go on our honeymoon before our 5-year anniversary. A week-long trip somewhere, just David and me away from everyone. Someday, Lord, someday. You are here and I'm so utterly thankful You are with me. Thank You, Jesus for Your faithfulness. In Your name I pray, amen.

God's girl,
Molly

March 3, 2013

God is so gracious! He just gave us $150 from my grandparents for Alex's birthday.

By the way, David is still looking for a job. We trust and pray He provides David with work soon. He's had three interviews and has two more interviews tomorrow. We'll see.

God's girl,
Molly

March 8, 2013

"Be still and know that I am God." Birds chirp in the background as I sit here in the stillness and quietness of a house where everyone is sleeping. The thought of new life comes into my head. I hear an airplane over my head. San Diego and the new life we will bring there—for Alex, for the people we will meet, and for us.

Life is new because Jesus died to bring the dead to living a new life. He brought David and me who were once so lost and miserable without Him to live with Him and rejoice in Him. I'm so thankful for Him, for Jesus who died on the cross and rose from the dead in order to redeem us.

I know that He is God. I know that in the stillness of my home, God is right by my side. Just like He was with me back in high school as I sat for three hours in the quietness of the desert. Just like He is with me now as I run and try to get our house ready for people over. Just like He is with me. I'm so thankful that He is faithful.

God's girl,
Molly

❧ ❧

I cried a lot last night and David comforted me. He took Alex out this morning and gave me this time to just be alone with God. Last night I cried because I'm overwhelmed by mothering Alex. I feel as if for so many reasons I'm a bad mom. David listened to my many fears and failures. He pointed out that the Bible does not say what it means to look like a "good/bad mom."

Alex is a sinner, and I can't keep expecting him to listen to me and obey me. God commands children to obey their parents, but they don't. They sin and so does Alex. I need to expect that. He will sin against me, and I will discipline him.

Even if he says he's sorry, I will put him alone in his bed for five minutes. All bad behavior requires some discipline, but when you're sorry about it there is often less punishment. David pointed out that Alex is a lot like himself. Just speaking to cover up the issue by saying you're sorry is still bad and needs discipline.

God's girl,
Molly

March 20, 2013

Thank You Lord for healing the woman who bled for twelve years, and for raising the dead girl to life (Luke 8:40-56). You helped them when they most needed You, and You helped us when we most needed You. Thank You for providing for us the checks and the tax refund money right when we needed it. Thank You for Your provision through giving David the job that will pay him in two weeks. Thank You that he's working from home. Thank You for helping us out financially when we would have had no money. Thank You.

God's girl,
Molly

April 17, 2013

Three years. We've been married for 3 years now. I'm more in love with David than I was when we said "I do" and more in love with him than I was when we first dated. I definitely love him more now than I did when we first met when I was nine. Oh, the married life—the joys, the sorrows, the blessings, the misunderstandings, the frustrations, the love, the patience, and the laughter.

God's girl,
Molly

May 25, 2013

Oh Lord, how I love the silence and stillness of our home. So peaceful. So calm. Thank You Lord that I woke up at 5:30 am and got to get away with You. I needed that time alone with You. I always need it, every morning. You're a fresh, daily reminder to trust You. Thank You that my parents have offered to help us move. Thank You that it's cold again. Thank You for giving us a friend to move in with in September. Thank You for so many things.

God's girl,
Molly

June 8, 2013

Help me, Lord, to truly trust You with providing for us. Help me to understand and let go of my pride, providing for us through my parents. You're moving Alex and me to San Diego a lot sooner than I thought, like in a few days and not in March 2014.

David and I had a rather large discussion last night about me freaking out about money. He pointed out the things that I just prayed about. He really misses me and wants to spend our last Saturday doing something special. I'm in denial about us being long-distance for a few weeks. *Lord, please sustain both of us while we're apart. Help me to understand Your brilliance, glory, and magnificence. Thank You for being glorious, and thank You for showing me a glimmer of Your glory.*

God's girl,
Molly

June 11, 2013

David and I are going through two different books about church planting, *The Church Planting Wife* by Christine Hoover, and *Church Planter* by Darrin Patrick. My favorite quote from each:

> No matter who you are or what kind of church planting work you're doing or what is going on with your church, you will face the decision daily: faith or fear? Dependence or independence? *Christine Hoover*

> In all the uncertainty and instability of church planting, we don't have to despair for He holds all things together. Rather than expending our energy attempting to control life, rather than trying to fulfill some false standard of perfection, we must instead cultivate a dependent heart. *Darrin Patrick*

I'm really excited about church planting. Though I expect the process to be long and weary—David will be gone often, my days will be filled with me cleaning our house, my husband will be critiqued and criticized, and a lot will be expected of Alex. Yet, God is calling David and me to plant a church in San Diego. We're following Him.

God's girl,
Molly Grace Mulano

June 12, 2013

"No one can serve two masters, for either he will hate the one and love the other, or he will be devoted to the one and despise the other. You cannot serve God and money." Matthew 6:24

"Keep your life free from love of money, and be content with what you have, for he has said, 'I will never leave you nor forsake you.'" Hebrews 13:5

"For the love of money is a root of all kinds of evils. It is through this craving that some have wandered away from the faith and pierced themselves with many pangs." 1 Timothy 6:10

"And my God will supply every need of yours according to his riches in glory in Christ Jesus." Philippians 4:19

I love being satisfied when we have enough money. Right now, we do not have more than $200 in both accounts, and $150 is due July 1st for our cell phone bill. I'm stressed, anxious about money, and worried that we won't have enough and will have to ask for Dad's help. I love the comfort that money gives. I love the calmness a steady income gives. I love money right now.

Oh Lord, I see now how I'm sinning against You by loving money. You said I can't serve two masters but have to choose between You and money. Help me be content with what I have. Help me be satisfied with You. Thank You that You said You're always with me. Purge me of this evil love of money. Help me to trust You that You will provide for us. Supply us with our needs. Thank You that You will not leave me and that I can be satisfied with You. In Jesus' name, amen.

God's girl,
Molly

October 3, 2013

God indeed provided for us...a friend paid our cell bill and covered it "as a gift." David nearly cried when I told him and I was touched too.

David went to Pastor Randy a few days ago to talk about fundraising, and left talking about planting a church. The funny thing is Randy wants David to partner with him in another church. David is floored because he's only been here in San Diego two months and we agree with everything the church is doing, and he's really excited about working with them.

What Randy wants to do is train leaders who plant churches. He's very organized—thanks be to Jesus—which they need. But Randy doesn't know David well, or me, and we're gonna take some time to get to know them first. They could pay David in about a year so he would need to find a job or fundraise.

I really don't know what I think of that. Still thinking and praying.

God's girl,
Molly

January 6, 2014

Dear Lord Jesus, I'm tired of waiting. Waiting to find a new car after ours was totaled. Waiting to find an affordable home, and where that home will be. Waiting, waiting, waiting. Thank You that patience is what I have to learn, even now when we're in San Diego. Thank You for Your love, grace, kindness, and compassion. Thank You that You are wise and always act in Your wisdom. Thank You for being gracious toward us. Thank You that You know when and where we are going to move. Please show us soon and please help me be patient while I wait.

God's girl,
Molly

March 13, 2014

David and I talked today about everything—and the answer is.... rest. Grrrr. Why does God want me to rest? I am a going type of person. We have wondered why the Lord has us here in my parents' home after five or six times we could have moved, and He prevented us from leaving. The job(s) fell through, our potential roommates fell through. David told me that he had applied to over 1,300 jobs in San Diego and none of them got back to him. Starbucks Corporate asked him if he wanted to work remotely for them part-time, which David has accepted. So, we're resting. Patiently. Waiting. I don't like waiting patiently, but Jesus wants us to wait and so we patiently wait.

God's girl,
Molly

March 16, 2014

We attend a wonderful church plant in San Diego that teaches us a lot about Jesus, as the gospel is preached nearly every week. We are very involved with the people of this church. One time I took Alex to the main pastor's house to play with his children.

The wife and I chatted about my story. As she listened, she said, "Maybe God doesn't want you to plant a church in San Diego." I was surprised by what she said, but I began to pray about what the Lord wanted us to do.

God's Girl,
Molly

CHAPTER 7

God's Plans

I woke up this morning and the following verse was on my mind: "I wait for the LORD, my soul waits, and in His word I hope; my soul waits for the Lord more than watchmen for the morning, more than watchmen for the morning. O Israel, hope in the LORD! For with the LORD there is steadfast love, and with him is plentiful redemption." Psalm 130:5-7

This sooo spoke to me. God's been speaking to me about how I need to wait on Him for moving out, being in San Diego, getting our own apartment, and everything else.

I opened my Bible to Psalm 9, 84, and then 130. The Lord spoke to me through every one of those Psalms. In 84, He comforted me through verses 10 and 11: "For a day in your courts is better than a thousand elsewhere. I would rather be a doorkeeper in the house of my God than dwell in the tents of wickedness. For the LORD God is a sun and shield; the LORD bestows favor and honor. No good thing does he withhold from those who walk uprightly."

God being my shield comforted me because He protected me from death when I had my stroke/heart surgery. And He shielded me from losing Alex when I almost had a miscarriage. He has bestowed favor and honor on me through the prayers and finances given to us in our first year of marriage. He did it the next three years through our parents and Josh and Samantha helping us.

Psalm 33:20—22 spoke to me: "Our soul waits for the LORD; He is our help and our shield. For our heart is glad in Him, because we trust in His holy name. Let your steadfast love, O LORD, be upon us, even as we hope in you."

I am hoping in Jesus now. Whether or not He provides enough for us to move out, I trust in Him.

God's girl,
Molly

March 20, 2014

We are visiting David's family in Texas right now, and after being around my cousin Iris who has a baby, I really want to have another one. David doesn't want to have a baby. So, we're not. But I really want another one! And I'm trying really hard not to cry. I'm having a hard time. I know in my head that God knows best and He has me not getting pregnant at the moment. And probably never. David is so worried about me and doesn't want me to die. I don't think I will die. But I don't know if my pregnancy was really difficult because of the stroke. Maybe it was or maybe it wasn't. I don't know. But tears are streaming down my cheeks and I don't know why.

Oh Lord Jesus, please help me! Help me to trust You with all my heart and to rest assured that You are in control. Help me, please, and carry me for I have no strength of my own. I love You Jesus and my life is Yours. Every day, every second of my life belongs to You. May it be as You have planned. But Lord, I want another child. Here is my desire—all that I have I give to You. May it be as You want—not as how I want. I surrender everything. In Jesus' name, amen.

God's girl,
Molly

March 21, 2014

After I journaled last night, I talked with Mom Mulano for a few hours. We hid away behind the fridge away from everyone else and I talked to her openly. Through tears, I shared what I had written. She listened and comforted me. We ended up talking over a lot of deep things. A lot of what I go through, she has too, and I knew that before I opened up to her. It was really good.

I texted David because he had asked me throughout the day if I was alright. It was midnight and I stayed up till 12:40 am to talk with him as we drove around town. He listened, and I opened up how I'm feeling. I mentioned my cousin's baby, and that when I held him, I made him smile. I had distanced myself from everyone, except the baby. I would only smile radiantly when he smiled.

Anyhow, the one thing David pointed out was that I'm exhausted being Alex's mom. I really do get tired with Alex. David thinks that we're supposed to be like Priscilla and Aquila in Acts. Just a part of the Gospel and not exactly the ones in the pastor position. But who knows, God may change us and direct us there. With that role from God, we'd be moving a lot. Which is why we can't adopt—because we won't be in the same city for a long time. He is also scared about me getting pregnant again because he doesn't want to lose me. And he could. But then again, I'm God's girl and so I'm here for His pleasure.

David loves me and loves it when we are involved in ministry together. David and I would love to take in older kids. But it's not as easy as filling out some form for that to happen.

So, I don't know what I want now. David made a lot of really good points that I didn't write about, but I'm processing them. *Lord, Your will and not mine be done.*

God's girl,
Molly

March 26, 2014

Dear Lord Jesus, please show us what it is that You want us to do now that Starbucks has offered David a full-time job if he moves to Dallas. Do You want us to move to Texas now? Do You want us to move into a studio apartment here? Do You want me to work? Please show David if you would have him stay in San Diego or move. We thought You wanted us to plant a church in SD but everything seems to be going south. Please reveal what You want us to do and please help us become the people You would have us become.

God's girl,
Molly

April 13, 2014

The Lord is clearly speaking to us about Texas. He spoke to David directly through reading Jonah. We both felt like we're Jonah and the people of Dallas are like the Ninevites. We didn't want to move to Texas before—I even made David swear to me that we wouldn't live in Texas filled with all the "nice" people, cowboys, and no ocean in the middle of Texas.

But we're feeling like we're supposed to go there. This past Sunday in church we were praying and, when the worship pastor read the Bible, he stopped in Jonah. He felt the Holy Spirit move to tell someone that they were supposed to love the people abundantly and then about how we have to go to some place and love them, even though it's like Jonah and Nineveh. David and I were floored. We talked to him about Texas, and now we're moving there!

Then today God spoke to us again through three different people. The first was my mom, and she said the Holy Spirit led her to a passage in Scripture that she shared with us—Deuteronomy 31:7, 8: "Then Moses summoned Joshua and said to him in the sight of all Israel, 'Be strong and courageous, for you shall go with this people into the land that the LORD has sworn to their fathers to give them, and you shall put them in possession of it. It is the LORD who goes before you. He will be with you; He will not leave you or forsake you. Do not fear or be dismayed.'"

And then one of our friends spoke to David and said something about us acting courageously. Another man heard our story about moving to Texas and he came up to me and said God gave him one word to tell me – courage.

God's girl,
Molly

April 17, 2014

Ahhh! We're moving to Texas in a month! It's so crazy.

Father God, please help everything to go smoothly. Help all we do glorify, please, and honor You; playing, eating, spending, saving, planning, packing, and living. Help David and me to trust You. Help us both to understand that You have everything planned. You want us in Dallas...I have no idea why yet, but You do. Help us to have faith in You. Help us to live lives so filled with Your Holy Spirit.

Thank You Lord that we made it four years today since our wedding! You are good to us all the time. We're alive still and You've placed us on this earth for a reason. Redeemer, here we are. We're Yours.

God's girl,
Molly

April 20, 2014

Thank You Lord that You gave David the wisdom to decide that he would move first to Texas and Alex and I would come later. Thank You Lord for helping me accept that. Please help me accept that joyfully. Please help us as we're apart for roughly six weeks to keep our eyes on You. Please help me be kind to my parents. Please help me be kind to Alex. Please help David be strong. Lord Jesus, our lives are Yours.

God's girl,
Molly

June 30, 2014

Thank You Jesus for David and the conversation we had.

I hate moving, changing locations, and meeting all new friends. I'm really tired. I'm selfish, angry, depressed, and I didn't sleep last night. We're staying at David's parents' house and there is no room—six people in two bedrooms.

And there are bugs everywhere!

I know that "the Lord's strength is sufficient for me for His power is made perfect in my weakness" and that God is working this out for His good will. And that the Holy Spirit is interceding for me right now. But I don't feel like it. I'm upset and just sulking.

God's girl,
Molly

July 1, 2014

Dear Lord Jesus, You seem to be putting me together with all single moms. I've been here almost two weeks and I met three single moms. There's also a home for battered women/single moms close to us. David really wants me to plug in there. It's funny because in Chicago, that's who I was mostly with toward the end of my time there. Single moms.

No wonder You told me to have courage. Courage to show them that Jesus is all that matters. Courage to admit that the Holy Spirit is at work in my life. I so prefer to be quiet and not up front but You have placed me here. I'm Yours, Father. Do with me as You please and help us. May we all seek satisfaction in You. Help me to love You more than I love David. Help me to help encourage these women to love You more than their lack of men. Help glorify Your name.

God's girl,
Molly

July 10, 2014

We're moving into a new apartment tomorrow!! And I'm sooo excited!

Thank You Jesus for allowing us to move into an apartment by ourselves and pay for it all by ourselves. Thank You Lord for teaching me that we need the Body to function and can't just be alone. Thank You Jesus for both of our parents and them letting us live in their homes. You have provided us with sooo much and I'm absolutely grateful.

God's girl,
Molly

April 4, 2014

I was in a car accident and I'm shaken up. God protected us all and Alex was farthest from where I was hit. Everyone's fine. "But this I call to mind, and therefore I have hope: The steadfast love of the Lord never ceases; His mercies never come to an end; they are new every morning; great is your faithfulness." Lamentations 3:21-23 is where my Bible was, and this verse is what the Spirit used to comfort me.

God's girl,
Molly

August 6, 2014

Well, I'm having a pretty bad attitude right now. Why? Because I'm a sinner and that's, I guess, what sinners do. Our wifi doesn't work, though David managed to get my phone to work on wifi...but it broke. David is home sick today, and my mother-in-law is on her way to take us to church because our car is still not working.

Why are we here, Lord? You haven't told me and I'd like to know. We're supposed to love people and be courageous—what does that look like? David was super excited after community group because they had mentioned they would like to get another person on board for leading a community group, and he's been wanting to lead one for like forever. Yet, Father, we only just got here and the pastors don't even know us that well...but please let it all work out where we lead a group.

Please draw all the people I've met here to Yourself and help us be a part of that. Please help me to have a positive outlook and realize that these trials are meant to draw me closer to You. Help me to, with confidence, draw near to Your throne of grace that I may receive mercy and grace to help in my time of need...which is right now. Thank You for sending me my mother-in-law—please increase her strength.

God's girl,
Molly

August 12, 2014

Our car is totaled, which is great because we don't have to pay extra since I was in a car accident. Thank You Jesus for paying our bills!

God's girl,
Molly

August 13, 2014

God is so awesome. Our car insurance company ruled our first car accident not our fault, which means AAA is going to give us the money back, and I think it's going to be $800 which is what we owe David's family. Yeah Jesus!

God's girl,
Molly

August 25, 2014

We got a car! God is awesome because we have a little money left over.

God's girl,
Molly

August 27, 2014

I have a ruptured ovarian cyst which is causing all of the abdominal pain, nausea, throwing up, and so forth. And the doctor wants to wait six weeks to find out if they have to do something to remove it. They don't want to do surgery because of my history. I don't understand why; I was already opened up once. What's a second time gonna hurt? Oh well.

Oh Lord, You know my body and my physical well-being better than I do. You know my body is aching. Please stop the pain. Please be glorified no matter what, whether it stops or not. Help me to sing and proclaim Your faithfulness during this time. You were with me when I had the stroke and heart surgery, and You are with me now. Thank You for always being by my side.

God's girl,
Molly

September 1, 2014

I absolutely love Alex at this stage. He laughs, smiles, makes noises with his trucks and cars, plays with "cat woman" (stuffed cat) and "batman" (stuffed dog), paints, draws, and puts his shirt on backwards.

Well, he just had a fit and purposely spilled water on the ground, so I have to go. But I do love him so.

God's girl,
Molly

October 4, 2014

Ok, so we have bed bugs in Texas now. Three states and we've had them in every state. Thankfully we caught it early so that they were only in our bedroom, not Alex's.

Dear Lord Jesus, please teach us whatever You have to teach us through this trial again. Thank You for sending me David as a husband.

God's girl,
Molly

CHAPTER 8

The LORD Provides

Over the next few years, I learned that the Lord provides for me. When I was in Jr High/High School I attended a young women's Bible study with Mrs. Linda. She taught us a lot of Scripture, but one thing I truly benefited from was studying the names of God.

One name in particular became real to me and that is *Jehovah Jireh*—the LORD Who Provides. The name *Jehovah Jireh* first appears in the Bible in Genesis 22. God tests Abraham and tells him to take his son Isaac and sacrifice him. Abraham obediently takes his son up the mountain, without telling Isaac that he will be the lamb. Isaac wonders what they were going to sacrifice and asked his father. Genesis 22:8 says, "Abraham said, 'God will provide for himself the lamb for a burnt offering, my son.' So they went both of them together."

God will provide. *Jehovah Jireh.*

Abraham had waited years for this child to be born. Years. Isaac was the fulfillment of so many promises. His mother was old, and by a miracle Sarah conceived. Here the Lord tested Abraham by asking him to sacrifice that miracle son.

I'm a mother and I know how crazy it is to think of killing, sacrificing, my own son. Yet, the LORD asked this of Abraham, and so he did. He placed his son on the altar, was going to kill him, and then the moment came. Abraham trusted God to provide the lamb.

The LORD stopped Abraham's sacrifice in Genesis 22:11-14: "But the angel of the Lord called to him from heaven and said, 'Abraham, Abraham!' And he said, 'Here I am.' He said, 'Do not lay your hand on the boy or do anything to him, for now I know that you fear God, seeing you have not withheld your son, your only son, from me.' And Abraham lifted up his eyes and looked, and behold, behind him was a ram, caught in a thicket by his horns. And Abraham went and took the ram and offered it up as a burnt offering instead of his son. So Abraham called the name of that place, 'The Lord will provide;' as it is said to this day, 'On the mount of the Lord it shall be provided.'"

God provided a ram instead of Abraham sacrificing his own son. Abraham trusted God to provide. He didn't know how it was going to work out. He couldn't see the future. He surrendered everything including the life of his very own son, letting go and letting God be in control. Hebrews 11:19 says, "He considered that God was able even to raise him from the dead, from which, figuratively speaking, he did receive him back."

I'm not saying that the Lord will provide everything you want and all you need to do is trust Him. He warns us of sitting lazily and expecting God to work everything out. Proverbs is full of warnings for sluggards and for habitual laziness. Colossians 3:23, 24 says, "Whatever you do, work heartily, as for the Lord and not for men, knowing that from the Lord you will receive the inheritance as your reward. You are serving the Lord Christ."

It's not in Scripture that God will make everything magically happen—make you wealthy and free of disease. No, there is a great cost to following after Christ. Luke 9:23 says: "And He said to all, 'If anyone would come after Me, let him deny himself and take up his cross daily and follow Me.'"

Say no to myself and yes to God? Deny myself? Take up my cross? Does that mean I can carry my cross necklace? Or does that mean a real, wooden, splintering, heavy cross? Daily. Cross. Follow Me. This makes me wonder if just being the "nice" Christian attending church on Sundays is actually carrying my own cross? I think this calling means so much more. Could it mean, daily sweating and sacrificing everything? Surrendering everything over to God, every moment of every day?

I still struggle with the Lord providing. I still struggle trusting the Lord, surrendering to Him again and again. As I write this book today, thirteen years have passed since I said "I do" and suffered that stroke.

One more comment before we get into this chapter of our marriage. To this day it is mysterious to me why I experienced such destitute times while David worked for prestigious companies. He never allowed me access to information about our bank account, our credit card statements or our tax returns. He would give me a tiny monthly allowance out of which to pay for groceries and gas and sundries.

No matter the objective reality of our finances, God used this time mightily in my life. I learned that when I ask Him to provide, He does. Sometimes He provides with money, sometimes He provides opportunities to learn, and sometimes He provides with "wait." But through it all, the Lord has always provided.

❧ ❧

A few of my journal entries starting at the end of 2014 showing how the Lord provided

December 30, 2014

Well, I ended up in the hospital a few weeks ago because I had a seizure. The meds have made me very tired. Thankfully David took off work to care for Alex and me, our church is helping us by paying our rent this month, and Dad offered to pay $300 for the hospital.

I'm just thankful to be alive. Why I am alive and here right now, I don't know. But I'm thankful. Thankful to be with David and Alex and that David went back to work yesterday. Thankful that Jesus is letting me stay and care for Alex. Thankful that Jesus is faithful and He is always here. Thankful that David loves me and God's love surpasses David's love.

God's girl,
Molly

January 2, 2015

Dear Jesus, thank you so much for providing for us all these years. I ask that You please provide for us again. The hospital stay cost $500 and David took time off to care for me. We paid the hospital bill and thankfully the church paid our rent. We just need food. Please provide us with some food to eat. I have $30 to spend on groceries for two weeks—make it work, please. Thank You Lord for providing us with a good doctor and healthcare.

I hate that we have to rely on people to pay for things. But Father, I have another doctor's appointment with my neurologist on Monday and David has to go to work over the next two weeks. I'm Yours, Lord. My body, my mind, my spirit, my time, my energy, and my bank account are all Yours. I surrender everything over to You. Here I am. Amen.

God's girl,
Molly

January 3, 2015

God provided again. I replied to a text that a friend sent, only I replied ALL which meant that I sent it to others as well. I was complaining in the text, and now I'm so humiliated and humbled. We were given more money through it to buy our food. My mother in-law also gave us some of her food.

God's girl,
Molly

January 20, 2015

Oh Lord Jesus, I'm so tired. And I think I'm done.

David will be working at home now; he has finally gotten the full-time Starbucks Corporate job they promised. Yeah!

God's girl,
Molly

February 12, 2015

Thank You for today and the peace I feel inside of me. Thank You for our new/ used washer and dryer and that I can wash/ dry everything in it today before the pest control people come tomorrow. Thank You for the food I am preparing for our city group tonight, all thanks to my mother-in-law and mom. Thank You for David and Alex. They are not perfect just like I am not, and I thank You for their imperfections. You provided!

God's girl,
Molly

February 27, 2015

Lord, please help me to trust You completely with our money. It seems like as soon as we have a little money, all of a sudden, things happen such as our washer not working or we have to pay for a bed bug treatment. Lord, I'm struggling to not freak out because we don't have a lot of money at all. Help me to rejoice in You. Help me be at peace as I try to present my requests to You with thankfulness. Help me to thank You for the little things.

Thank You that it snowed here in Texas. Thank You that You have covered our basics, such as a roof over our heads and food tonight to eat. Thank You that we bought a real bed, not just the mattress on the floor like we've been living with. Thank You for our washer and dryer. Thank You for loving me. Thank You for being here for me right now when I'm about to freak out. Thank You that I can rely on You always. I need Your help. Please give me Your strength. Help me, Lord, for I have no strength of my own. Thank You for remaining faithful.

God's girl,
Molly

March 27, 2015

Dear Lord Jesus, please help me know whether or not I should go talk with a counselor or pastor about David and my past. I'm just uneasy about it. We didn't "do" anything, but a lot has happened to us since we said "I do."

I don't know, Lord, but I feel like I want to talk with a pastor about David's ADD and manic depression that not a lot of people know about. As David's wife, I feel like I am held responsible for this depression, which I am not, but it sure feels like it.

Father, I don't know why we're here, but You said to go to Texas and take courage. For what?! I don't know. I merely am here. I feel this weight of our past five years laying on me, and more than that of the sixteen years that we've known each other. I knew he was manic depressive before now. Father, I want You to make everything all better, but You won't and You chose to make this side of David just like the stroke/heart tumor side of me. Father, am I ever going to know why?

Oh Jesus, thank You for redeeming us. Thank You for transforming us from the inside out. I praise You for dying on that cross and for taking our multitude of sins.

God's girl,
Molly

April 3, 2015

Thank You Jesus for this group of believers that came to our house Wednesday night. Lord, thank You for the chance to open up our home and serve them. Thank You that they are coming in the future. Thank You for speaking to me through that. I felt like I was Home with You. As if no matter where I'm at, just being with other believers makes me feel like I'm Home. This world is temporary but Heaven lasts forever. You are my eternal Father who loves me sooo much. I feel relieved. And at peace. Thank You.

God's girl,
Molly

April 23, 2015

Thank You Jesus for giving David a big raise at Starbucks!! Yeah! Thank You that we didn't get in on the benefits and free food for Texas and that we now have enough money to provide for us! Hallelujah!

God's girl,
Molly

April 30, 2015

Dear Lord, I feel so awful because last night David and I were talking and he convicted me of viewing my identity as a stroke victim and not as Jesus.' It's so true. I want to make sure that everyone knows that I had a stroke so that they won't wonder 'What happened to her hand?' I feel like that is the greatest part of who I am, not that Jesus saved me.

Father, how do I change that? You were my Redeemer even before You healed me. The people here don't know I had a stroke until I tell them. They think I'm a normal person. Forget the fact that at night, when I'm tired, I can't remember which words go where when I speak. They honestly don't know and that makes me feel uncomfortable.

And if I only explained they would understand. Father, I want the people here to know that You healed me, saved me from physical death. You also saved me from spiritual death too, back when I was little, and do I not want them to know that too? So that You can save others? Jesus, I'm weak and tired and just want to give up. Please help me? Be my strength. Please help me.

God's girl,
Molly

May 28, 2015

My husband is depressed, like maybe clinically depressed. His work is great because they are offering to pay for him to see a psychologist. He is taking a leave of absence, which is paid, for the next 12 weeks. I pray, pray, pray for him to find hope in Jesus.

God's girl,
Molly

May 30, 2015

I'm just too tired and exhausted from Alex, my stroke/heart surgery, and these meds I'm on because of this seizure. And now David is diagnosed with severe depression and I'm worried about him. I just talked with a friend, and she listened as well as counseled me.

She said that God has protected David through crazy circumstances. And God has sustained David through situations that would break most people. God has safeguarded David and gotten support in place. She told me to trust that Jesus understands David's sorrows and the Holy Spirit will counsel him.

God's girl,
Molly

June 10, 2015

I was worrying about how we were going to pay our rent, buy Alex clothes for school, and eat in the meantime. Our landlord sent a notice that we'd be evicted if we didn't pay, but we did pay on the 1st. Then I looked at the grass and noticed flowers blooming and I heard birds singing. The Holy Spirit used that to remind me of Matthew 6:28—33:

> And why are you anxious about clothing? Consider the lilies of the field, how they grow: they neither toil nor spin, yet I tell you, even Solomon in all his glory was not arrayed like one of these. But if God so clothes the grass of the field, which today is alive and tomorrow is thrown into the oven, will he not much more clothe you, O you of little faith?
>
> Therefore do not be anxious, saying, 'What shall we eat?' or 'What shall we drink?' or 'What shall we wear?' For the Gentiles seek after all these things, and your heavenly Father knows that you need them all. But seek first the kingdom of God and his righteousness, and all these things will be added to you.

God is good, always good. I don't know what is going to happen, but the Lord promised to be there for me and I know He will be. David is not committing suicide today; he is on meds that will help him. I am ok, struggling to be ok. But God is good and He will provide. As He clothed the flowers, He will clothe Alex. As He fed the birds, He will feed us. We're trying to figure out our payment, but at least I'm calm now that God reminded me of His righteousness.

God's girl,
Molly

July 1, 2015

Dear Lord Jesus, thank You for this time I get to spend alone. Thank You that David is actually awake and prompted me to go out for like four hours. Yeah! It's been a hard few weeks with David sleeping or being dizzy. Thank You that we got paid yesterday for David's term of absence. Thank You that he feels much better as compared to the last four years.

Thank You for caring for me and for being faithful. Thank You Father for taking care of me and for Your provision. Thank You that our city group sent us home with a ton of food. I really like our new city group. Lord, please continue to guide us as we are here in Texas.

Show me where You want me as Alex goes to preschool in August. Thank You Lord for Your provision with Uncle paying for our plane tickets to San Diego in August before Alex starts school. I haven't been home in over a year. You are good.

God's girl,
Molly

August 16, 2015

We're in San Diego! God used this morning to refresh me. His presence is evident in San Diego among our friends. David and I both have had a really hard time being in Dallas and we needed our 'gathering' to point us to Jesus. He never said it would be easy, but He did promise to be faithful. Our Lord is so faithful and loves us so much—even when we're faithless to Him.

When we took communion, David told me he felt as if the Spirit told him to let me pray about whatever is on my heart. I broke down and said that I miss Jesus. I miss the sweet intimacy and joy of knowing Jesus together in community.

David let me know that he thinks this year has been about waiting for God, waiting on the Spirit to move. He thinks the time has come for now we are to act as foot soldiers, not as the leader, moving toward community together. We don't know what that looks like or how or when, but we wait for the Spirit to lead us further.

God's girl,
Molly

September 3, 2015

God is good. Alex is in preschool. YEAH!!

I went to a training for New Life Ministry last Saturday and it stirs my heart to hear of what other women are doing to rescue and restore women who have been sexually exploited. I'm currently in the process of applying to become an advocate, which is scary but I'm doing it because the Lord laid it on my heart.

He will give me the courage to get to know and love the women who have been sexually exploited (sex slaves/sexually abused/former prostitutes). I'm excited to meet the women, love them, and offer them hope.

God's girl,
Molly

September 21, 2015

Dear Jesus, our car broke down last night in our parking lot. I have been praying for about two hours about the car, David's job, our finances, Alex and me walking to school, and the New Life advocacy program, Lord, I'm tired now. Please be glorified through making it all happen.

God's girl,
Molly

September 24, 2015

> So we do not lose heart. Though our outer self is wasting away, our inner self is being renewed day by day. For this light momentary affliction is preparing for us an eternal weight of glory beyond all comparison, as we look not to the things that are seen but to the things that are unseen. For the things that are seen are transient, but the things that are unseen are eternal.
>
> *2 Corinthians 4:16-18*

David was in another car accident while riding his bike, and he has a concussion. Our car broke down and we still don't have the money to fix it. I'm tempted to look outwardly and be overwhelmed, but I just read this scripture which renews me. These momentary trials are afflictions which hurt, but they too will pass.

I can look toward Jesus, my eternal God, who will never change. This Jesus is eternally loving to me. This Jesus is eternally merciful and forgiving toward me. This Jesus is the same Jesus a week ago when our car worked.

I'm thankful He is constant because I'm unstable. I'm thankful He is holy because I'm a sinner saved by His grace. I'm thankful He is strong because I'm weak. I'm thankful the Holy Spirit intercedes for me because I do not know what I need prayer for right now. I'm thankful to be alive because I wouldn't be except for our Father who rescued me and David countless times. I don't see Him, but I trust He is with me and carrying me close to His heart.

God's girl,
Molly

September 26, 2015

Someone just offered to pay us for David resting! It's funny because we have $150 and we were supposed to get more money yesterday but we didn't. Anyhow, someone just called David and offered to pay for our car to be fixed (I posted yesterday's message to Facebook and they had seen it). Then they talked to David, and I think they're also paying for our rent!

I don't know exactly, but either way they're paying for something and I'm grateful. Thank You Jesus for providing for all of our needs!

God's girl,
Molly

October 13, 2015

THANK YOU JESUS THAT DAVID HEARD BACK FROM AMAZON!!! He's sending them an email back with his availability for a Skype interview. They offered him a job he did not apply for, like Technical Support II, and he wants to make sure he can do the job. *Lord, please help David do the job and help them to like him.*

God's girl,
Molly

October 20, 2015

When I lack trust in God and we don't have money, I get mad at everyone. I so quickly forget the gifts we have received—like how my mother-in-law paid for our groceries yesterday, how we've managed to pay our rent this month and next month, how we've paid all of our bills out of the money someone gave us to fix our car, how we've been able to take the bus places through David's work, and how countless people have given us rides.

I do believe, Lord, help me overcome my unbelief. Turn my bitterness into joy. Turn my anger into love. Turn my not trusting into trusting. Thank You for providing so much for us over the years and even this past month. Please continue to provide. May David get the Amazon job and may it pay by November—in enough time to pay our bills that month.

God's girl,
Molly

October 23, 2015

God is so good. I gave $2 on Sunday to the church because we don't have a lot of money right now. I then flipped out because our money seemed to be going faster than I thought. God gave David the interview today and he did really well! And then he opened his bag and found a note and $200 in it! Our Father has provided!

God's girl,
Molly

November 1, 2015

A new month has begun and I'm singing praises to Jesus. Why? Because He is good and He provides. Provision has always been a touchy subject for me, but I know that God provides and "every good gift is from above." And He has given us abundantly more than we deserve time and time again.

David hasn't been paid by his job since August and that isn't the way I foresaw it. I want to be able to pay our bills. I had to cancel our insurance because David doesn't have cash coming in and we can't pay for our car to be fixed or insurance. Then again, he is getting paid by our church to run sound, so this month's rent was covered, and our groceries.

I bought all of our groceries for two weeks and only spent $33, including conditioner and laundry soap. I've seen our food last for so long because God provides. We have never gone hungry and have always had a roof over our heads. Why? Because Jehovah Jireh—the LORD provides and I'm thankful today.

God's girl,
Molly

November 2, 2015

Lord, we have $0.56 in our account, nothing in savings, and we just paid the rent. I'm scared, Father, help me to trust You and help us to have enough money. Please provide the job at Amazon or another job to call back and hire David immediately. Please help me not to worry because I offered to work but David said no. Help me to trust You and act in a way that pleases You.

God's girl,
Molly

P.S.

Thank You Father for providing for us yet again through someone at our church. You truly are amazing.

Father, You have revealed how I put stuff and toys and Christmas gifts above You. I've been greedy and I ask Your forgiveness. We do not have any money to buy Alex Christmas gifts this year and I was stressed out about that, and being unable to give other people gifts.

But Lord, as I sit here and think, You **have** *shown me what it means to rejoice in You through the generosity of so many and through the attitude my child has, thanking everyone for giving him his favorite toys over the four years of his life and for being so generous to give away even his favorite fire truck to a child with few toys.*

I see our Jesus sacrificing His life for a bunch of selfish people. I see Jesus thanking God and overcoming the world. I see my sin and I praise Jesus for taking that sin and dying with it on the cross. I see Jesus coming up out of the grave and telling us to go and make disciples because He is with us.

I see Jesus. And I rejoice in Jesus. Thank You Jesus for filling my heart with You.

God's girl,
Molly

November 23, 2015

Praise Jesus, Amazon said yes!!

They will fly David out to Seattle January 5th for two weeks, and pay him more than double what he's currently making.

Thank God for making this possible. I never imagined that he could make this much money. Please Lord, help us be wise in our spending and generous in our giving. Father, You have provided for us abundantly! Help me Father to worship You and not money.

God's girl,
Molly

December 13, 2015

Thank You Jesus giving me everything—Yourself, eternal life, the Father's faithfulness, the Holy Spirit interceding for me, the wonderful love of my husband, the embrace of my son, a roof over my head, food in our cupboard, my feet that can walk again, my right hand that can write again, my mouth that can speak again, and so much more that You give us.

I'm sorry that I've been so selfish, greedy, and self-righteous lately. Help me to give to You without expecting a reward. Take my money and show me where You would have it go. Lord, we don't have much but the little I have I give to You.

God's girl,
Molly

December 20, 2015

Dear Father God, it's Christmas week and I'm at peace. David and I had a difficult time last week with my hurting him and David being mad. We did forgive each other. Teach me to trust him with our money. Thank You that You gave us this money. Ever since September David hasn't been paid and we've managed to get by because You send money. Help me to see You always giving us what we need to live off of even when David gets his first paycheck from Amazon. Thank You for keeping us from spending the night in hospitals this year and for keeping me healthy. Please continue to do so.

As I look around the house this Christmas season, I see three stockings that David's grandma made for us before she died. She died when I was in 7th grade, and yet she made us two stockings because she knew we would get married out of love. Your peace and joy filled her heart to the end, which made David dedicate his life to You. We don't have a lot to fill our stockings with this year, but that's okay. It means more to me that we're here together—David, Alex, and me.

On my birthday in three days, I don't think I'll get many presents. At first, I was disappointed when I thought about it. But now, I'm not because David promised to be with me and we're taking Alex to the bakery. We'll be doing such amazing things together this year such as seeing Star Wars. Then David's mom is cooking some of my grandmother's most delicious recipes for my birthday meal, and a favorite dessert. I'm content and at peace.

All of that is nothing compared to Christ and what He suffered for me. That truly satisfies my soul—trusting Jesus is more than enough for me. I make mistakes, we don't have a lot of money, yet Jesus died for us and rose from the dead so that we might be saved through His grace. He came down at Christmas time to live in this broken world. *I pray I will always remember that You love me so much, and showed me Your mercy by lying in a manger and later dying on that cross.*

God's girl,
Molly

CHAPTER 9

His Grace is Sufficient

Through trials and suffering, I learned that Jesus is most important. I did not always live like this was true, but Jesus' grace kept me going. In Scripture, Paul speaks about grace a lot.

The one passage in particular that stood out to me at this time in my life was 2 Corinthians 12:7-10. Paul suffered great trials, yet boasted not in that but of his weakness. Some people say it was his eyesight that bothered him. No matter what his weakness was, here is how he described it: "...a thorn was given me in the flesh, a messenger of Satan to harass me, to keep me from becoming conceited. Three times I pleaded with the Lord about this, that it should leave me."

I too had a weakness—my stroke and the effects thereof. I begged God to take the effects away, but He didn't. At this point in my life, I felt as if I had to tell people as soon as I met them about my stroke because I was afraid they would think poorly of me because of my hand, memory, and the way I limped. The Lord used this passage to teach me that His grace is sufficient in my weaknesses.

Even though I was physically suffering, I learned to rely on His strength. I began to learn to depend on Him. Second Corinthians 12:9, 10 says, **"But he said to me, 'My grace is sufficient for you, for My power is made perfect in weakness.' Therefore I will boast all the more gladly of my weaknesses, so that the power of Christ may rest upon me. For the sake of Christ, then, I am content with weaknesses, insults, hardships, persecutions, and calamities. For when I am weak, then I am strong."**

January 7, 2016

Lord, I miss David a lot and want to cry. He left for Seattle on Monday and won't be back until January 25th. My mom is coming for the second week. I'm excited that she is coming. I'm weary, Father, and Alex has been difficult today (and yesterday). I'm stressed about tomorrow—it doesn't seem like I'll be able to get everywhere on time.

So please help me get to Alex's immunization at 8am, get to school, meet Sheri (my new "New Life" woman) at 11am, then back in time to pick up Alex from school at 2pm. Please help me to trust You and not look at David for my fulfillment. You fulfill me. Help me to trust that You are the only One who is enough. Help me not to cry because David is gone. Thank You that David is able to text me all day—it's better than when he moved here to work for Starbucks. Please carry me.

God's girl,
Molly

January 8, 2016

The Spirit refreshed me last night when we went to our city group and a friend prayed for me. He prayed specifically that God would reveal Himself to be my provider, protector, and lover and that I would love Him more while David's gone. I read through the New Testament passages on "fear not" and these words in I John 4:18, 19 came up: "There is no fear in love, but perfect love casts out fear. For fear has to do with punishment, and whoever fears has not been perfected in love. We love because He first loved us."

It's funny because God has brought the words 'no fear,' 'perfect,' and 'love' into my mind this past week. I'm reading a book on being a perfectionist, and how Jesus already loves us perfectly. I pray that this truth would be real to me.

Yesterday as I was reading, Jeremiah 17:7, 8 stood out to me:

> Blessed is the man who trusts in the Lord, whose trust is the Lord. He is like a tree planted by water, that sends out its roots by the stream, and does not fear when heat comes, for its leaves remain green, and is not anxious in the year of drought, for it does not cease to bear fruit.

As I read these words, a picture came to my mind and I started to paint it. I saw a tree with big roots planted by a stream with the light shining down on it, and its leaves were bright green. I pray that I will trust the LORD that way, trust that He loves me perfectly.

God's girl,
Molly

February 7, 2016

Last night I was overwhelmed, ashamed, anxious, and burdened. David and I talked about it, and he said I do not like asking for help. I don't really. I've had to ask for help a lot without us having a car that works. Yesterday I had to ask someone to drive me twice and I cried because I felt like I was being a burden to my friend for driving us to church. I like helping other people and serving them, but when they serve me, I don't like it. David and Alex are the only people I want to help me out.

Anyhow, at church this morning God spoke to me because Pastor Jim said something about Jesus being the answer to everything—that He offers us hope, grace, and peace in Him despite our sufferings. That's just what I needed.

Our house is still a mess. I don't have a car so I still need to ask people for rides, but I feel better now because I'm asking Jesus for help with everything. The Holy Spirit gave me His peace today. And I also talked with my friend about all of this.

God's girl,
Molly

February 11, 2016

Lord, I feel like crap today—mentally, emotionally, physically, and spiritually. Please hold me and make me holier like You.

(A little later) I asked everyone through text for a ride and we'll see if anyone answers. If not then we'll find some other ride. I read the Bible about "complaints" because I thought it was evil to complain, but David told me it's not.

Anyhow, I realize now I can complain about situations, but I need to also give thanks. *So, thank You Lord that I feel this way. Thank You for remaining the same always. Thank You for holding me tenderly. Thank You for walking with me as I walk Alex to and from school every day.*

God's girl,

Molly

February 12, 2016

It irritates me that I'm not more loving to Alex, that I'm not the "perfect mom." Alex irritates me sometimes. He's loud and our neighbor downstairs complains to me about the noise. She even called me a "not-so-good mom because you can't control your son." I know that I shouldn't take it as fact, but it does hurt.

Also, my sister is trying to have another baby now. It makes me kind of sad because she is so kind to her little girl already, and she is trying to have more kids. I wanted four children. Four. I only have Alex. and he bugs me at times. Other times I love him and we have the best time. But he's bugging me today.

I injured myself today. Just tripped and fell, spraining my fingers on my right hand and twisting my right foot. Figures it would be today of all days. Anyhow, my mother in-law picked up Alex from school.

I feel useless, which ironically is just what God and I dealt with all those years ago when I had the stroke. I'm reading a book by Amy Baker called *Picture Perfect* which deals with all of this stuff. My life is not picture perfect at all. I know that. I'm not saying it will be but I want it to be. I want it to seem perfect.

Father God, I need Your help. You are in control, and You have led David and me to not have more children. Please help me to accept that. Please help me to realize that You planned everything. I made plans that did not happen. You are good though, and I thank You.

Thank You for Your compassion for me though I fail again and again. Thank You for Your grace and mercy which help me get through each day. You are the Good Shepherd and You gently lead me, Your sheep. You can see the path behind, and the one in front of me. You know what's best. Thank You for knowing best. Thank You for planning best. Thank You for knowing that this season of my life has me having Alex. And that's enough. He is enough because he is what I have.

God's girl,
Molly

February 19, 2016

I realized today that I am a glory thief. I've been reading the whole concept of glory thieves in *Picture Perfect.* As I'm lying here in bed, I realize that I wanted David to be a pastor. I wanted him to be the one telling people about Christ and leading them to Him.

I wanted to be his wife, the example for many to follow. I wanted my testimony to be shared and my story to be told so that many would come to Christ and sing my praises. I wanted to pray for the church and see the people grow in number and in depth.

I wanted all of these things. But they were not in God's plan for us. He wants to be glorified. He deserves to be glorified. Whereas I had wanted to receive a little praise, a little "Wow, you went through all of that...and you're doing great!" I didn't want praising Jesus to be their only response.

Oh Lord God, who is in heaven and who is worthy of all praise. All praise, not some "thanks" or "great job." Worthy. Oh Father, You are so worthy. I am not worthy of all praise. You are. Your Son is. Oh Jesus, thank You for being glorified on the cross. Thank You for being glorified in who You are—my Shepherd, my King, my Life, my Love, my Everything. You are worthy of all praise. So, I praise You. I praise You for Your majesty, glory, splendor, grace, kindness, compassion, love, mercy, forgiveness.

Will you please forgive me for robbing You of glory? I'm truly sorry. Lord, it's funny how you often send me to do that which I don't want to do. But I do it because You told me to. I obey You most of the time. But I do not obey You joyfully. Lord, please forgive me. Help me to point everyone to You—not to me. In Jesus' name, amen.

God's girl,
Molly

February 28, 2016

I just saw a picture of a couple I know going away for the weekend and I got jealous. Jealous that David and I decided not to go away this year for our anniversary because we bought a new dryer that actually dries our clothes, unlike our old dryer that stopped working. I said it was fine that we didn't go away, but now I want to go somewhere with him. I'm coveting a vacation. We spent our money on moving to Chicago, back to San Diego, and then to Dallas. We followed God in obedience as He clearly wanted us to move. Yet, I'm longing for a vacation. Most people can't afford to travel or go on expensive honeymoons. I know all this, but it's hard to watch other people travel while I'm stuck in Texas.

Father God, please forgive my covetousness and envy. Please help me to be okay with not going on vacation. Help me to accept Your plan as wonderful and perfect—knowing that following You is hard and worth it because You are the way, truth, and life. Thank You for Your love, mercy, and grace. Thank You that You know best. Thank You that You are perfect and I am not. Thank You Lord that our friends got to go on a vacation. Thank You Jesus that we got a new dryer that actually works and I don't have to go up and down the stairs. Thank You so much for that.

Thank You that David is married to me and we got to watch a TV show last night. Thank You that we got to follow You to Chicago and San Diego and Dallas. Thank You for the countless people we ministered to while we were there. Thank You for the people who ministered to us. Thank You that earth is our temporary home and that heaven is ultimately where we are going to live forever. Thank You that there is no more crying there, nor death, nor eternal suffering. Thank You that You are good and ultimately our money is your money. Do with us as You want. I trust You.

God's girl,
Molly

Praise Him, Not Me

About six years ago,
I had a stroke and heart surgery,
Of which I did not know,
The extent that my body had on me.

The night I had married my best friend,
I lay hospitalized,
Fearful that my life would end,
Thinking clearly but unable to verbalize.

The doctors found a tumor in my heart
That had broken off in my left brain,
Causing the stroke to start –
The thorn in my side emerged.

Paralyzing me,
On my right side,
Is how I was to be,
Including my muted voice.

Robotic, open-heart surgery,
Within a month, they performed,
Removing the tumor within me
That would have caused my soon death.

Through many doctors and nurses,
God spared my life,
Through many long months
My right side is working again.

Jehovah-Rapha, the LORD who heals,
Is the One who healed me,
Yet He is also Jehovah-Mekoddishkem,
The LORD who sanctifies me.

As I moved my foot, hand
And began to speak again,
I prayed that He would not
Allow me to forget again.

My mind forgets words
Like the simplicity of "chair,"
My hand can write slowly,
But at times it closes up.

I can walk again,
But I cannot run fast,
Or ride a bike, or skate, or
Play a sport, except come in last.

I'm tired, I'm feeble,
I'm handicapped-
BUT GOD-
God saved me.

He sent Jesus to die
In my place on the cross,
Redeeming me with His death
Restoring me through His new life.

His grace is sufficient for me,
For His power is made perfect
In my weaknesses,
So, I praise Him.

Praise Him, not me,
For He is good, glorious, kind,
He adopted and adored me,
I am the daughter of the King.

"The thorn in my flesh"
Is my stroke and the effects on me,
For when I'm weak,
Christ is my strength.

So I'm reminding myself
Not to view me as a stroke victim,
But to see His grace that saved me,
My identity is in Christ alone.
-MGM March '16

Amy encouraged me to post this poem to Facebook, and I did last night. A ton of people thanked me for writing, and my mother in-law, Lillian Mulano, posted this response:

Beautiful tragedy, wonderful wounding, regally redeemed. That night changed so many things, sweet Molly, but your story was not over, it was just beginning. I am inspired by your strength, strength that is not your own but points to One greater and by your unfailing faith in the goodness of One who loves you more than I, more than your (at the time) brand new husband, or your own sweet momma. Your poem brought it all back and brought tears to my eyes, tears of joy and hope in El Roi, the God who hears. Thank you for sharing. He is glorified so sweetly through your life.

Rest

Go, go, and don't stop,
Is the house dirty or clean?
Toys, dishes, food made...
Real rest I long to glean.

"Rest in Me"
I hear Him say,
But truly what does He mean,
Does He say it every day?

"Come to Me,"
He whispers gently,
"And I will give you rest,"
He states humbly.

Alas, I respond that
I am heavy laden,
I have been carrying my cross,
David's too and Alex Aiden.

Yet my soul seeks rest
So to You I lay my burdens down,
As I sigh in great belief
Of Your sustaining love for me.

-MGM March '16

May 2, 2016

Father God, you seem to say no a lot lately. I wanted a car to drive and You said no. I understand why David thinks it's unwise for us to go ahead with the Toyota Corolla purchase. It would cost $3,000 additional to fix it. That would be $5,000 and we don't have that money. Yet, I cried and prayed the whole way to Alex's school.

Do I just have to keep on walking Alex back and forth from school? Do I have to be submissive to my husband? Do I have to rejoice in this area of my life? What are you trying to teach me? Patience? Stillness? Joy in this suffering? Again? Peace? Love? Quietness?

Are you trying to calm me with Your perfect love? Am I supposed to thank You? Thank You for not fulfilling my dreams of having a car to pick Alex up from school. Oh Lord, a friend moved in with us two weeks ago. She has the same car I've wanted. Thank You that she offered me her car this afternoon to drive and pick up Alex. But I needed to clear my head and walk. And Alex is here now.

God's girl,
Molly

May 3, 2016

Dear Father, what is up with my life? It seems like every month this happens where I get excited about something and then it doesn't happen. College. Marriage. Stroke. Heart surgery. No honeymoon. Alex. Transient ischemic attack. Almost losing Alex three times. Chicago. David losing his job. San Diego. David Pastor in San Diego? Nope. David trying to find a job. Moving to Dallas and we're still here. Still no honeymoon/vacation. Seizure. David's depression. Lack of money. No car. David being out of town for work.

There have been lots of good things, an abundance of You showing up to shepherd, provide, comfort, protect, shower us with grace, mercy, kindness, and love us. I acknowledge You; I praise You for being so good to us. I thank You for these past six years. The joy and the sadness.

But Lord, the hardships I have endured have really been hard on me. I'm weary and I really want everything to be perfect. But this world is far from perfect—let me tell You. Yet, You know this.

Thank You that Your Spirit sees everything. You see the battles in my heart. You hear the wrestling in my mind. You know the struggles in my body. You are intimate with my soul. I am Yours, and You are mine. Thank You Jesus for loving me, for showing me love through the difficult times. Satisfy me this morning with Your steadfast love O LORD.

God's girl,
Molly

May 29, 2016

Lord, please help me as we move. I'm so tired and I don't have the energy. Please help us all. Thank You that no matter where we move to, You're always there. Thank you for moving us into my friend's duplex. Thank you that Alex can be as loud as he wants and we have no downstairs neighbors so it doesn't matter if he runs in his room. Please help David and me sleep well tonight. It will be a long day cause we're both helping out at church.

God's girl,
Molly

June 16, 2016

Dear Lord Jesus, I'm kinda nervous about my surgery next Friday. They say if I want to have children again, I can have surgery again to make that happen. Oh Lord, I want more children but David said no. So I submit now and will have the surgery. Please help it go well. Thank You that Alex was born and that for now you have closed my womb. Thank You for David and that he will hold my hand.

Help me to have courage to tell everyone tonight at our city group. I don't even know if it's "appropriate" to talk about, but I really do need their support. Thank You for the countless people who prayed over my heart surgery. That was a surgery that we weren't sure I'd make it out of alive. Even with the heart tumor, if they hadn't found it, I would have died within 3-5 months.

But here I am. All praise be to Jesus who showed the doctor my heart tumor and who performed the surgery. Thank You for seeing all things, knowing and caring about all things. Even a bird flaps her wings and You know when it falls. Thank You for taking care of me my 26 years and that You promise to look after me always. Thank You that You will hold my hand throughout the surgery. Thank You. In Jesus' name, amen.

God's girl,
Molly

June 25, 2016

Well, I had the Essure surgery to make sure we don't have any more kids. I'm at peace about it. I have one child. Never thought I'd only have one kid, but I do.

God's girl,
Molly

August 20, 2016

Dear Father God, so San Diego again? We had countless people ask us if we're moving back, and why not, because we do make enough money to live there. David and I talked about moving back when we were on a date night. We've talked about moving some place for a long time—anywhere but Texas. Every time You said no and that's why we're still here.

This time David was talking about work and how he would have to fly out for a day as opposed to flying 5-7 days to Seattle for work. He's been gone so often because of work—it seems like he's gone for a week per month, or every other month...a lot longer than we expected he'd be gone when he first started. There are Amazon people in San Diego that he can meet with...he wouldn't be so lonely. And we'd get more money if we moved because it costs more to live in California than Texas.

But what about why we're here? Have You taught us enough? Have You used us in people's lives here? Have we loved the people here? Is it wise to move back home to San Diego? Will Alex be alright moving again? He loved the ocean and even boogie-boarded for the first time.

David and I have a lot to do this year—Alex's in school starting Monday and David needs to find someone who can replace him for running sound. It's good that we have another ten months till our lease is up. David said we'll take till January to pray and decide about moving. We'll save up money. That way we can move if necessary.

I'd love to move and be home in SD. But we'll see…whatever God says we will do.

God's girl,
Molly

August 25, 2016

I'm afraid of David and Alex dying, that You would take them away from me and I'm gripping onto them for dear life. David leaves for Seattle the day after tomorrow and I don't want him to go. I love him. You could have taken him countless times over the years between his past life and car accidents. And yet he still lives.

So basically, why are all three of us still living? Thank You for letting us live. I love David and Alex so very much. Thank You for their lives. Thank You for our life. Thank You that David and I get to live forever with You. Thank You for always being there for us, to hold us and to comfort us, to redeem us and to be faithful, loving, merciful and gracious to us.

I pray that You will redeem Alex, that You would save, sanctify, and restore him. Lord, You have indeed sanctified David and me over the past six-and-a-half years, and even the past sixteen years of our lives. Oh Lord You have. I cannot count how many trials that You used to mold us—please break us into mirrors that reflect You. We're not perfect, far from it. I'm emotionally and physically tired. I'm signing off now.

God's girl,
Molly

September 23, 2016

I've felt pretty discouraged today about my life and ministry and not feeling like I'm having an impact on people. Two families Alex was close to at school moved, two people I knew committed suicide last year, a dear friend is just doing alright but nothing's changed. I welcome people on Sundays but it just seems like a joke and I'm not actually helping people.

I told David all of this and he asked if I was being faithful to what God's called me to obey. I answered yes. He said I have no control over how other people respond. I'm just called to be faithful and let God handle the rest.

David said I'm ministering to more people by praying for them than if I was a pastor's wife. I pray every day. And I also have a prayer meeting at my house every other week where 1-7 people come and we pray for an hour.

David also mentioned words of affirmation may be my love language but they are also damaging to my wanting to seek approval of people, and wanting to know that what I said encouraged or instructed them. Though I feel as if it were not worth it, I'm called to be faithful and that's what I'm doing.

I'm still processing that. To be faithful. Year after year. No spiritual gift is higher than another, like thinking that being a pastor makes you more important than just a person serving. I'm just a person serving, but I'm serving Jesus through welcoming, through trying to minister to people. Only God knows what kind of impact I am making. The Holy Spirit is moving in ways I cannot see.

God's girl,
Molly

October 20, 2016

Dear Lord, my mind is going a hundred miles per hour of what I should do or not do, and be or not be. Alex has asthma and I've had to run around a lot because of the doctor's appointments and getting his medicines. Today is going to be a long day. Thank You Lord that You already knew why Alex was having trouble breathing. Thank You for the health care we have with David's job.

Thank You that they paid for everything, all $400 of Alex's medicines. We are eternally grateful that You provided David with this job and the crazy health benefits. Thank you that Alex's health was bad this year while we're under his company health care and not last year when we had nothing. Continue to help him breathe. May this medicine be the right kind. Thank You for always providing. Thank You for always loving.

God's girl,
Molly

December 23, 2016

Dear Lord, I'm 27 years old today. 27. *May this year be pleasing to You. May I be holy like You are holy. May I be pleased with You above all else, and seek my satisfaction in You. Thank You for giving me David and Alex. Thank You for David's family. Lord,*

I pray that as we transition to San Diego that we would do so smoothly and not roughly—that we would be kind and generous to people here and not mean and rude. I pray that You would help me in particular. I so often close myself up and feel secluded—I don't want that to happen.

God's Girl,
Molly

December 31, 2016

A lot of people have said that 2016 sucked, and at some points it did, but honestly it was the most rewarding year for David and me. There were definitely hard points with David being gone so much for work and Alex having fits.

I was finally able to admit I have difficulties because of the stroke and could just say no to meeting with people when I was physically unable. I wasn't involved in as many activities as I would have liked, but I feel a lot better than I did in past years.

David got a job that actually paid him and he was able to provide us with a comfortable home, and pay for my medical expenses. Alex went to school and enjoyed new friendships. As this year ends, I'm actually content as described in Philippians 4:11-13.

> Not that I am speaking of being in need, for I have learned in whatever situation I am to be content. I know how to be brought low, and I know how to abound. In any and every circumstance, I have learned the secret of facing plenty and hunger, abundance and need. I can do all things through Him who strengthens me.

God's Girl,
Molly

CHAPTER 10

Honest Lamenting

Honest lamenting was something that I learned at this time in my life. What does it mean to lament honestly? Grieving is tricky. I'm no expert. Losing someone is hard, whether that's a baby or your grandma or a friend. I grieved because of several people dying or walking away from the Lord. The psalms ministered to me during this time, especially Psalm 42. I also went through another very hard trial myself.

January 11, 2017

I wish someone somewhere had gone through what I'm going through and written a book saying "In six years you'll be tired and forget everything because of x-y-z." Then it would make sense why my mind is muddled up. I would really like to know what is going on with me medically. I would like to know, like in a handbook, what a 20-year-old who had a major stroke caused by a heart tumor struggles with? I'm tired. Way tired. I don't know why. Is it because of the stroke? The doctor said I would have more energy when they removed my heart tumor. But that's not happening.

Lord, I don't know anything but You do. You know why I'm tired. You know why I'm losing my memory. You know why my right hand hurts and curls in. You know why I limp. You know why and You care. Thank You for caring. Lord, please forgive me for being jealous of other people I see who get to drive to school. Please help me to let go of that sin. Help me to clean up our house and then rest.

Thank You for David who sent me to bed early last night. Thank You that he's still married to me after all these years with my stroke messing up my mind. Thank You for his job that pays well. Thank You that I don't have to worry about money anymore. Thank You for taking care of us all along.

You are great, mighty, righteous, and holy. I praise You. I praise You despite my weaknesses. I praise You even though I'm tired, even though I don't want to move my legs. I praise You.

God's girl,
Molly

January 20, 2017

Oh Lord, I'm a little scared about losing David's mom. It looks like she has cancer of some kind again. Help me to be there for David, his mom, and everyone in their family. Help me to be patient and wait for David as we head to the hospital. You decided to take away Lillian's mom and brother, but you let her and her sister live. All four of them battled cancer. Now Lillian has it again.

Father, please let her live longer on earth. But, Father, if it is Your will to take her now, help us to be strong and grieve. Help us Lord, for we are weak and cannot survive this on our own. Lord, you allowed me to live after my stroke/heart tumor. You helped me through the many nights at the hospital. Help Lillian too. Help her rejoice in her sufferings. Help her to be strong. Stop the pain, Lord.

God's girl,
Molly

January 25, 2017

Well, David's mom has cancer and I can't sleep—I've been up since 3:30 am. Lillian has lung cancer that has spread to her bones and skull. It's incurable and you can't cut it out.

We're not moving to San Diego but are staying here to help Mom. She can't move or drive. She's in so much pain. David was depressed and sat in his room alone two weeks ago when she was having problems with her lungs. He's 'fine' now, just busy with running errands since Mom can't now. We always knew she was going to get cancer again—I just didn't think it would be this soon.

God's girl,
Molly

January 27, 2017

Alex has the stomach flu and is throwing up a lot, so we're not taking him to school or my mother-in-law's house. I guess this is God's way of saying I need to slow down.

I'm very sad for Lillian and yet envious because she gets no more pain soon when she goes to heaven. I don't like pain and cancer sure gives pain.

God's girl,
Molly

February 7, 2017

I think we've told the most important people, and everyone else will find out about Lillian through someone. I'm very drained emotionally.

Alex and I just had a hard conversation. He was complaining that life isn't fair and that I hate him and am mean to him. I asked him how many people have moms who have strokes. I then asked him how many people are young and have strokes. When I told him the answer it blew his mind—he thought that everyone's mom went through what I go through every day.

I explained to him that it's not 'fair' what I went through. I groan about it, but keep going. I walk and talk because God is good. Then we talked about how He has a plan that is better than our plan. I had the stroke to teach me that life isn't fair. Alex settled down afterwards.

God's girl,
Molly

February 23, 2017

Mom Mulano and I just had a really great conversation as I was reading her Scripture. We talked about how she came to Christ in 6th grade and re-dedicated at the end of high school. Then she commented that she wished she had been faithful from the start, like the way Jesus had saved me at a young age and I've always followed Him. She doesn't regret her life, but she wished it were different.

I said that's funny because I always love telling other people about her and David's testimonies. She was surprised. I said that God redeemed her and David and brought her through so many things, and that I find great joy in hearing those tales. I follow Christ, but every day hasn't been the 'best day,' and sometimes I go through different seasons.

She was reminded that we're all a tale of Jesus' ultimate redemption. He has redeemed us all from broken lives and saved us from whatever sin we choose to cling to rather than cling to Him. Our God is pretty amazing.

God's girl,
Molly

February 25, 2017

I've been praying that David and I will be able to go on vacation for our ten-year anniversary in 2020. We have not been gone for more than a night since we got married. Sometimes it's really hard to be married to someone who is manic depressive. But I've known him for seventeen years now and I love him so much. I pray that we will grow closer emotionally and mentally. It's hard taking care of his mom but I love her and love giving her everything I have.

God's girl,
Molly

March 12, 2017

Lillian has stage 4 lung cancer metastasizing quickly.

Dear Lord, Lillian's not doing well at all. Are You going to take her from us soon? Can You please ease her pain? Please miraculously heal her. Or take her home to be with You. Guide us and show us what you want us to do. I'm sitting with her as she sleeps and everyone else is at church. Thank You Lord for allowing my parents to come. Thank You Lord for the great time they're having with Alex.

It's hard to watch my mother-in-law suffer. I know I suffered through the stroke/heart surgery. It was hard for David, our parents and family, basically everyone to watch me suffer. But this we do, suffer as our bodies do not want us to be whole. I still suffer handicap with my right arm, and sometimes my right foot stops, and I forget everything.

But Lord what is it You wrote? Rejoice in suffering? Rejoice in Jesus. Take joy knowing my Redeemer. Take joy having Him know me, love me, be gracious to me. I don't always take joy in those things. I grumble and complain, as I'm sure Lillian is doing. Our bodies are weak. But inside is Your Holy Spirit which has power and is strong.

Please help us both. Encourage Lillian to endure the pain and push through. Comfort her in her pain and unease. Remind her of Your promises. Remind her of Your goodness, compassion, love, and mercy. In Jesus' name I pray, amen.

God's girl,
Molly

March 23, 2017

Yesterday was really hard for me. Inside I was weary, frustrated with everyone, not joyful, and emotionally drained. I was taking care of my mother-in-law who has to have someone with her 24/7. She is in pain, as the cancer has infected every single bone in her body as well as her lungs. This morning I read all of Lamentations 3, and verses 17-27 especially speak to my soul:

> My soul is bereft of peace; I have forgotten what happiness is; so I say, "My endurance has perished; so has my hope from the LORD." Remember my affliction and my wanderings, the wormwood and the gall! My soul continually remembers it and is bowed down within me. But this I call to mind, and therefore I have hope: The steadfast love of the LORD never ceases; his mercies never come to an end; they are new every morning; great is your faithfulness. "The LORD is my portion," says my soul, "therefore I will hope in him." The LORD is good to those who wait for him, to the soul who seeks him. It is good that one should wait quietly for the salvation of the LORD. It is good for a man that he bear the yoke in his youth.

God's Girl,
Molly

April 14, 2017

This week I had prayer on Monday and went to our city group on Thursday. David's out of town and I needed the fellowship. Today Alex and I went to Mom's house. He's actually out of school for Good Friday. Tomorrow's shopping day, then David comes home, and Sunday is Easter at Mom's house, and the following day is our anniversary. Man—it's a lot.

God has been working on my heart. Sometimes I'm doing great and trusting God and other times I throw a pity party. Last night was really refreshing as I got a chance to talk to my friends. And Monday was great as my friend and I prayed for countless people. Hebrews 12:1-3 has been a reminder lately to look to Jesus and not at myself.

God's girl,
Molly

April 25, 2017

From the mouths of babes God gently whispered in my ear to love my enemies. Alex and I were supposed to have people over today and they backed out. I was irritated with them because this wasn't the first time they'd canceled, and I hate it when Alex is disappointed. He cried when I told them they had canceled.

However, I told him he could go to the park. There was a little boy at the park playing soccer by himself, and I encouraged Alex to join him. They both had a blast. When we were walking home, Alex said that he didn't laugh at the boy when he tripped and fell because he chose to be nice and kind to him. He also said that we are to be nice to everyone, according to Martin Luther King Jr. and Jesus—who said to love our enemies.

It was at that point that I heard Jesus whisper that I too am to love my enemies, and people who have wronged me.

God's girl,
Molly

❧ ☙

Lillian is not doing well. Her spine has fractures because of the cancer tumors. And she has more fractures too. She can't walk, so we have to pick her up to put her in the wheelchair to take her to the restroom. She hasn't been able to move since February, so we have to move blankets, and move her feet and legs, and pillows. She's so feeble, but she keeps smiling.

The doctor did radiation, and the cancer in her lungs, bones, and blood should have gone away, but it's growing.

Oh Lord, I don't want you to take her home now. It's been just over three months since she was diagnosed with cancer. But Father God she's in so much pain because of the chemo/ broken bones. I pray that You would give her wisdom to decide whether You want her on hospice or not. I would go on hospice, but I'm not Lillian. Help her to let go of us, her family, and help her to hold onto You. You are good and faithful and amazing. You hold her tightly. Lord, please comfort all of the family and friends as we grieve. Be our peace and comfort.

God's girl,
Molly

April 28, 2017

Lillian chose hospice. *Oh Lord, please help us.*

David and I just went out for our 7th year anniversary. He's having a really hard time with his mom dying. Just angry and tired and trying to help everyone.

God's girl,
Molly

April 29, 2017

Dear Lord, here I am. I surrender to You. Do with me as You desire. I'm weary and don't have any strength of my own to keep going through this trial of the past seven years. I'm burdened for David, and I want to fix everything and make it all better: but I can't. Help me to not be torn down by that thought.

I pray that I would think of You, Lord, and the difficulties that You went through when Jesus came down to earth. Help David and me both come together as one, with the unity that You designed. Help us to bring You glory.

Help David not be so bitter, but help him to forgive. Allow him rest today. Help Alex and me get along well and help me guide him closer to You. I pray that tomorrow as we go over to Mom's house that we would bring peace and not division. I pray that the family would decide what hospice is best for Lillian. I pray that David would be okay with their decision.

God's girl,
Molly

May 18, 2017

David's mom passed away today. She died five minutes before we arrived. God's timing is perfect because Alex is little and I don't want him to remember her suffering. David is driving down from Chicago. I had to call him and tell him that his mom died.

Oh Lord please intercede for us because I have no strength of my own. Thank You for helping me get here safely. Thank You for bringing Mom Home to You. Please help me be strong for Alex and help me to grieve. Thank You that my mom is coming up here on Monday.

God's girl,
Molly

May 19, 2017

God's timing is so perfect. He worked out everything. Today Alex stayed home from school because his grandma had just died. I was crying because of her and then I remembered that some of my friends had asked to do stuff for us/offered their help. So, I asked for meals to help us get through the weekend. They of course jumped on the opportunity to help and I have meals till Tuesday.

I honestly don't think I'd be able to cook for us because everything in the kitchen reminds me of Lillian and I just cry. One friend brought me food and snacks today, and she brought so much that I was able to feed other people too.

Funeral planning was tonight and as I was getting everything in the car, which one friend had lent us the day before, another friend pulled up in her car and gave me a bunch of bags full of puzzles for Alex, snacks for him, food that he likes, paper plates, cups, silverware, dry shampoo, mints, tissues, and so much more.

I just about lost it, overwhelmed by my Savior's love for me. He knew what I needed when I needed it. Friends had asked me if they could bring meals for me but I didn't say anything until today. God knew I needed it now when I don't have the time or energy to cook for us. He knew to surround me with loving housemates who comforted me by coming over to talk last night and bringing us food today. He knew and I'm so thankful. So thankful. I'm so thankful He cares, loves, and meets our needs. I love Jesus. And He loves me too.

God's girl,
Molly

June 1, 2017

I'm at a tea shop and it's raining outside. My mom took Alex out to celebrate his kindergarten graduation today. She told me to stay at the tea shop and not rush back. I'm glad because I need the alone time. My tea tastes weird but I don't mind because I'm without people. There have been sooo many people in the past four months since Lillian got diagnosed with cancer. I'm glad to sit in the quiet with funky tea.

It's so weird that David's mom died. Every day I think of her when I'm in the kitchen or just randomly throughout the day. Sure, I've only been married to David for seven years but, honestly, it's been seventeen years since I met the Mulanos. There are sooo many pictures of Lillian and me when I was little. So many.

It struck me that the timing for her death was perfect because if this had happened ten years ago, I wouldn't have been ready. There's no way.

I'm glad I'm calmer now. My stroke/heart surgery helped me handle Mom's cancer better. Even David was offering his dad advice. I'm so thankful my mom was able to fly out here and take care of Alex because, honestly, I don't know if I could have. I miss Lillian a lot.

God's girl,
Molly

June 2, 2017

David and I talked last night for a while. According to him and the research he's done, I only have 10-20 years to live. At first, my eyes got teary but then I was at peace. It makes sense because since December/January my speech has dramatically decreased and my right hand is almost permanently closed. I'm fine to die young. I've lived a long life and am ready to go Home to Jesus. This morning I read Isaiah 55:8-11 and it was perfect:

> "For my thoughts are not your thoughts, neither are your ways my ways," declares the LORD. "For as the heavens are higher than the earth, so are my ways higher than your ways and my thoughts than your thoughts. For as the rain and the snow come down from heaven and do not return there but water the earth, making it bring forth and sprout, giving seed to the sower and bread to the eater so shall my word be that goes out from my mouth; it shall not return to me empty, but it shall accomplish that which I purpose, and shall succeed in the thing for which I sent it."

God's girl,
Molly

June 5, 2017

Oh Lord, I'm so tired and weary of grieving.

My heart's broken for David and the bitterness he feels regarding "the church." We talked for a long time last night, raised our voices occasionally, and I cried towards the end.

Yesterday morning, he didn't want to go to church and we went to the zoo instead. He talked about how all he does is play with Alex and take care of me. Which is so not true but I can see his worry. I had told him no for being on the road, and other people had told him no for planting a church.

I think we need to go to counseling. I asked him but he doesn't want to.

God's girl,
Molly

June 28, 2017

I'm trying to process everything. David is unsure of his faith and has major problems with the Church (capital "C"). My mother in-law just died of horrible cancer. I'm here and I think I'm either being attacked right now for some reason with all of these changes, or my life just sucks real bad.

I don't know what to think right now—but help Jesus! I can't do this anymore. I can't. I don't have it in me. Please be in charge—it's so much easier when You're in control. Please give me wisdom in knowing who I can talk to about all of this.

I still believe in Jesus. I still believe that He came down to earth to bear my sins and He died for me. And He died for everyone. My faith has not been shaken, but boy am I weak. I cannot do this—live this life on my own. I need Jesus' help, now more than ever.

Oh Lord, please help me. Please give me Your strength. In Jesus' name I pray, amen.

God's girl,
Molly

June 28, 2017

Thank You Lord for helping me through our city group. They listened to me talk and they're going to help with Alex next week. Thank You for helping David and me be closer too.

God's girl,
Molly

July 24, 2017

Oh Lord, what do I do? My husband doesn't know what he believes. He doesn't believe the Church. His family is a mess and so is mine. Please help, Father. After my mother in-law died, I was grieving her loss, and still am, but there's so much more going on than just her death. It all came after she died.

I can't live for Christ and be surrounded by so much darkness. I need Your help. Thank you for the church and that they have helped me through this time. Thank You Lord for carrying this burden for me because I don't have the strength to carry it on my own

I remember a friend saying she read that passage about groaning and the Holy Spirit groaning for us. Please groan for me. Fill me up with more of You. Help me to know when to speak/act/do whatever You desire. Help me to pray for my family that they would know You, deeply, intimately, personally. Help them to repent of their sin and turn toward You. Show them mercy, please Father, I beg You.

Thank You for being gracious, merciful, faithful, kind, loving, and just. I still believe, help me overcome my unbelief

God's girl,
Molly

July 31, 2017

According to David, my life expectancy is 1/5 that of normal people because I had my severe stroke. It's even less than that because I had my TIA, second mini stroke. I didn't realize that until yesterday when David said that. I'm forgetting things more easily now. I can't drive. I forgot my pin code in the grocery store. I forget words so easily.

I know that my life is not my own, but for Jesus to do with however He pleases. I may live to be 100 or 40. I don't know. But I trust God to use my life however He sees fit. I'm glad actually that my life will be shorter. I'm way tired and ready to go Home. I'm ready and eager to be at the feet of my Savior. For now, I must wait. And serve Him however He sees fit. I pray a lot and more so now than before.

God's girl,
Molly

August 7, 2017

Psalm 42 is my prayer today. I'm so weak and tired and my soul is cast down. God is faithful but I can't see Him. I know He's with me but everything around me tells me He is not.

Help me remember You, remember Your steadfast love, remember that You are worthy of all praise, remember that You are my Rock, remember that my salvation belongs to You. Help me to find hope in You.

God's girl,
Molly

Have Mercy

Have mercy, O Lord,
Forgive those who hate,
mock and are bored
by Your beauty O Lord.

Have mercy and grace
on those I love with my heart,
help them finish the race
with their eyes set on Christ.

Have mercy, not judgment
on people weary from running,
Help them find contentment
In Christ & not themselves.

Have mercy.
-MGM July '11

September 6, 2017

Grief is so hard. We buried Mom's ashes yesterday. Today David turned 29. It's hard. Yesterday afternoon we all ate, cried, and laughed together. It was so sweet—all of us just sitting there talking. The past two or three weeks have been hard on me. I think it's because I'm alone and have time to think about David's mom.

I think it has also been hard because I'm anticipating my own death and grieving for Alex and David. I know it's not now, but it'll be here sooner than we all expect. Yesterday I was very forgetful and I had trouble speaking. Today not as much.

It's hard. So hard because David doesn't know what he believes about God and death and if Christianity is right. I love David—that hasn't changed. He still loves me. I'm so grateful that he has a job and pays our bills, because I'm unable to help at all. David and a friend have been taking care of Alex; walking him to/from school because even walking is hard for me now. We went to the zoo and normally I could walk for three or four hours but this time I was really tired after ten minutes.

Oh Lord please comfort us and enable me to continue on.

God's girl,
Molly

October 17, 2017

I prepared a speech for David:

"My parents offered to pay for our tickets to San Diego anytime. Here's what I'd really like—if we traveled over the beginning of January to see them. Then I was thinking that we could go on a cruise, just the two of us.

"Cruises are cheap and they leave right from San Diego. They're perfect for me because I can just go at my own pace. There's also a bar and my aunt and uncle used to get unlimited passes for the bar so we could save money, and you could always get a drink when I go to bed. You and I can rest and see the ocean, and eat delicious food. I would like to use my/our $700 birthday/Christmas present on it."

He said yes! We're going on a cruise!!

God's girl,
Molly

Chapter 11

The True Cost

There's this girl who David kissed, and my pastor accidentally told me because he thought David told me already. I'm mad at David and that girl. "Just a kiss," David said. She's staying in our house because "there is nowhere else for her to go." I want her gone. Arrrrrrrrgggggghhhhhh! *Lord, please help me be kind to her and David.*

November 10, 2017

My college friend Susan is here and I'm sooo glad she came. David flew her out here. I had an MRI done yesterday and a brain scan too. It was my fifth MRI, but this time it only took twelve minutes. My fourth neurologist in Texas is going to look through everything and we have an appointment next week.

I've only slept 3-7 hours a night all summer. I've been more forgetful, apparently even forgetting whole conversations I've had with David. I tried so many sleep drugs that the doctors were going to do a sleep study on me. But then I caved and ate a weed brownie by David's suggestion, and I have been sleeping 10-11 hours. I am also on three antipsychotics. I haven't slept that well EVER. I feel so good, but I'm still forgetting things.

Susan and I talked yesterday about my eventual death. I really don't know when God will take me Home. I have to trust the Holy Spirit to intercede for Alex, which is hard. Susan started crying during that conversation.

I have prayed to God to give me another year or two because it's too much for David to lose me and his mom at the same time. I know nothing and God knows everything: I pray that He will use my life however He sees fit.

God's girl,
Molly

November 13, 2017

Susan and I talked a lot. We talked about my stroke and the suffering I'm enduring now. My right hand is in pain. I can't sleep unless I take three antipsychotics, and then I occasionally sleep a solid 8-10 hours. My mind is disappearing. I can't think straight. Early in the morning is the best time for me to talk to people, but this morning I forgot how to say so many words. David says I forget full conversations that I've had with him and Alex.

In the past, we had hundreds of people praying for me to live, praying for the heart surgery to go well, praying for me to recover from the stroke. David said no people were allowed to visit me in the hospital other than my family. I did not understand it then and I was lonely—wanting people to come.

But now I understand it entirely. I cannot handle so many people. At home I have to go upstairs and be alone when Alex is talking too much, or our friends are over and I get overwhelmed. I can't focus on what people say if the radio is on. Too much stimulation makes me go bonkers and have to retreat upstairs, so I watch TV a lot. I used to be ashamed of that, but now I'm so exhausted that I don't care. I'm tired. I'm weary.

Jesus has been my refuge and fortress, protecting me from spiritually getting injured. Physically and mentally, though, I fear that I'm melting like a stick of butter in an oven. So many people wonder if God is their shelter when they've been abused sexually, mentally, or physically by a parent or stranger. Where is God when a child is kidnapped and tortured? Or a girl walking home is cat-called and raped? Or a baby doesn't live past their first birthday? They wonder if God is their comfort when they lose a parent, child, or friend. I've wondered. I've been up late at night questioning His goodness, grace, and protection. Why did this happen? Why did my mother in-law die of cancer having all of her bones broken? Why did she have to endure that? Why am I suffering as I am?

My cousin Iris and I are studying Job through a book that talks about having hope in God. In Job 1:21, how Job can say, "Naked I came from my mother's womb, and naked shall I return. The LORD gave, and the LORD has taken away; blessed be the name of the LORD"?

Job lost everything—his children, livelihood, money, health. He didn't have the Bible to read, or the internet to communicate to lots of people, or a pastor to pray for him. And yet Job said, "Blessed be Your name," and he meant it.

At the beginning, 7 ½ years ago, I too said, "Blessed be Your name, for You gave me a body before and You took away all of my strength when I had the severe stroke." But oh, it's hard to say that now. I sometimes wish I didn't have the stroke. I sometimes wish God had someone else tell their story to encourage people, or direct people, or reprimand people. I sometimes wish I could play the piano with my right hand. I sometimes wish that I'd had a check up on my heart eight years ago so that none of this would have happened.

I like to look at the ending of a story to see how people end up. Job sure had a hard life. The people in his life tried to be his friends, but their advice and opinions didn't help him. It's interesting how God responds by challenging Job, and Job confesses and repents.

I confess that I have been proud and scared and anxious. I don't "despise" myself, and that could be my pride, but I too, like Job, have lost a lot. God has a plan and nothing I say or do can change that plan from happening. My stroke happened. My mother-in-law died. I lost my nephew and brother before they were born. And somehow, I believe that God is still gracious to me, and merciful and kind and loving and good.

God's girl,
Molly

November 15, 2017

God You are good. Thank You for the prayers of Your people at our city group tonight. Thank You that You know everything that's going to happen.

God's girl,
Molly

November 18, 2017

Well, nothing came up on all my tests, which is exactly what David was afraid of. They gave me some medicine for forgetting things and ordered more OT and PT. I had to change my diet and stop drinking alcohol because of this medicine.

I'm having a hard time and I'm crying in bed alone right now. It hurts and I'm praying for the meds to work, but I realize that God has me sitting here in this trial for a reason. The trial is not my pain, but David's lack of faith; that he doesn't believe in God now. It's brought me so much spiritual pain and emotional sorrow. David is so stressed. He was super stressed and worried over the past few months that I was going to die. He's stressed about his job. He's stressed about pretty much everything, including our cruise.

Then it dawned on me that I'm supposed to help him regarding that stress. Only I don't know how. I can tell him to trust God more but he doesn't believe there is a God to trust. I can pray, which is something I haven't been able to do lately because my memory has been fading so fast.

I pray that David will realize that You are in control and You are God. I pray that David will trust You, that You will help him to see that You created the meds that he is on to help him not be stressed. That You are the God who is above anxiety and fear and worry. That You are the LORD who heals, who restores, who redeems, who created everything, who sees, who is my Shepherd, who is Peace, who is there, who is our Refuge, who is our Fortress, who is our Shield, and who is our Strong Tower. Thank You for being all of these things.

God's girl,
Molly

December 7, 2017

So much is on my mind. David's been depressed lately. And manic. Plus, I have to get up, get ready, and take Alex to school. Thankfully I have enough energy for that. I'm not making fancy meals anymore, but thankfully the guys don't mind. The main thing that has been on my mind is David's salvation and my entire extended family's future if they don't believe in Jesus. It's hard on me. I believe, still, but so many in my family do not anymore.

Oh, life is so hard and messy. It was so much "easier" two years ago, but then again, if they never knew Jesus in a real way then I guess it was just as difficult. Occasionally people "faked fine" and pretended that everything was normal when it wasn't. I've tried to be honest about my struggles, but some people said "Oh you're so 'perfect' and I'm sure you don't mean that," when in fact I did.

I tried and was impatient both then and now. I struggle with impure thoughts and vain obsessions. David's too busy worrying about whether or not I'm going to live. My grandfather had another stroke, so he's not doing too well.

I beg God and plead with Him to change everyone's hearts and He doesn't. My family still doesn't believe in Jesus. Nothing ever changes. I'm tired physically and emotionally and spiritually. This is my life. I can't sleep at night. I pray that I will trust God to work everything out, but honestly don't think I do trust Him. Trusting Him is something else I've struggled with for a long time. I have to actively trust Him every moment of every day. Thanking Him for keeping me alive despite all odds. Thanking Him for keeping Alex alive despite all odds. We're here for whatever reason the Lord sees fit.

My life is Yours, Lord Jesus. Here I am. The past is Yours, as well as the future. Do with me as You see fit. Help me to be Your hands and feet as I tidy up the house today. Thank you for allowing me a little bit more energy. Thank you for waking me up early in the morning so that I don't hear anyone and get to sit in the quiet. Thank You that it's quiet now while Alex is in school and David's still sleeping.

Thank You Lord that I get to enjoy You in the quiet and stillness. You are with me even now as You were with me back in high school. Thank You for Your faithfulness and love and compassion. Thank You for Your mercy and grace. Thank You that You are just, and the time will come one day when we're all going to stand before You. One day, it'll be my turn as it was Mommy M's turn in May. I miss her so much. Will You kiss her for me? I'm so thankful she's with You and You have healed her. I long for Your touch to make everything be well in my body. But now I suffer. I wait. I long. I pray for You to make me better, to make me a better person and change my soul to glorify You.

God's girl,
Molly

Posted this to Facebook/Instagram on December 12, 2017

This Christmas I have cried so many tears. I've sobbed more often than I'd like. My mother-in-law is gone and I miss her terribly. I'm finally realizing what it will mean for me to be gone—away from my little boy and loving husband. As my body slowly fades, I'm forgetting words. I have been up at 3 or 4 am, tossing and turning. Four antipsychotics don't seem to put me to sleep. Our house is a mess.

People outside are saying "Merry Christmas," putting lights up, and buying so many things for the holiday. I think about "Jesus is the reason for the season." He was born so many years ago. He, the High and Mighty, laid down everything to come to earth to be born. Helpless. Weak. Wordless. Jesus had to be taught how to hold a cup. He had to be taught to say "Mama." He had diapers, his bottom had to be washed again and again. So humbling, yet encouraging because I too am helpless, weak, and wordless.

December 13, 2017

David and I had another great conversation, but this time we dug deeper into my heart issues. The reason I don't respect David and don't trust him is because of fear. I fear he is going to die and not provide for me. I fear he is going to end our marriage and not take care of me. So I control everything that I can control by asking questions, again and again and again. I want answers now.

I fear that God isn't going to provide, and I don't trust Him with all my heart every moment of every day. Why do I fear? Why do I not trust David and respect him? Why do I not trust God to take care of me? Why do I fear that those close to me will die? Why do I fear every little situation that I'm no longer in control of? I don't know. But God knows.

God's girl,
Molly

December 14, 2017

I read and meditated on Psalm 56 today—I pray this verse for both my mom and me: "When I am afraid, I put my trust in You. In God, whose word I praise, in God I trust; I shall not be afraid. What can flesh do to me?" Fear has been a big part of my life recently. This passage says not to fear.

Oh Lord, help me not to fear, but to rely on You and not rely on my own understanding of life. Help me trust You with everything because You know what's going on with my life. You wrote my story. You are the author and I'm just a page in Your beautiful plan.

God's girl,
Molly

December 15, 2017

Fear. My life is scary because I can't clearly communicate my thoughts. I think them just fine, and I write fine, but verbally it's not all there. I pause and think of the word before I can say it out loud. And often I just stand there trying to think of words. And they don't come when I'm really tired.

The perfect love of Jesus is the opposite of fear. I know that He loves me, but do I truly understand, grasp, and comprehend the love of Christ? Do I truly know His perfect, holy, righteous love? Do I understand that He will love me forever?

I pray for the people who have had strokes, heart surgeries, and who are in the hospital every time I pass it on my way home from walking Alex to school. I pray that they would be healed by You emotionally, spiritually, and physically. That they may know Your presence. May the doctors and nurses be Your hands and feet.

God's girl,
Molly

December 21, 2017

We're in the ER because Alex got a LEGO up his nose. He's crying, poor thing. On Saturday he had multiple ear infections, so we went and got him medication. I guess God wants us back in the hospitals for whatever reason.

God's girl,
Molly

December 23, 2017

> "For My thoughts are not your thoughts, neither are your ways My ways," declares the LORD. "For as the heavens are higher than the earth, so are My ways higher than your ways and My thoughts than your thoughts."
>
> *Isaiah 55:8, 9*

Oh, thank You Lord for the time I got to spend today in Your Word! Thank You that Your ways are unlike our ways. I would have written my story much differently from how You have written my story. Yet it's not about me anyhow, but about You and Your glory. Help me sing and proclaim You. Thank You that Your Word accomplishes what You purpose it to, and succeeds in what You sent it to.

Thank You that You are God and Lord of everything, that I can have peace in knowing You. Your peace. I'm not afraid of people dying and leaving me defenseless because You are my good God who ordained everything.

I'm not afraid of my loved ones not knowing You because I pray that one day they will know You, love You, and taste Your goodness. Whether You answer that prayer Yes and they too will one day sing Your praises, or they curse You to their death—I still praise You. In this moment I have joy in You.

Thank You that I don't belong here on earth, but with You in heaven. We wait for Your return. We wait for You to transform our bodies to be like Your body. I so long for that! My physical body is so weak now. I'm forgetting things left and right. My mind is slowly fading away. You promise that one day You will take this decaying body and make it new, make it like Your glorious body. Oh, thank You! Thank You that Your Word is sure and steadfast. I can trust Your promises because You always keep them. You are good, glorious, righteous, faithful, loving, kind, and true. Thank You Jesus for 28 years of life on this earth. Today's my birthday, and You have given me the best gift ever in Your Word this morning.

God's girl,
Molly

February 5, 2018

God is good, gracious, and glorious. I'm still broken. I'm tired. But His love astounds me. I just read Nancy Guthrie's book, *Holding Onto Hope*, and love the following quote:

> I don't want to try and change God's mind.
> His thoughts are perfect.
> I want to think His thoughts.
>
> I don't want to change God's timing.
> His timing is perfect.
> I want the grace to accept His timing.
>
> I don't want to change God's plan.
> His plan is perfect.
> I want to embrace His plan
> and see how He is glorified through it.

Yes Lord, I accept my stroke. I accept Lillian's death. I accept my lack of sleep. I accept that Alex is my only son and I don't have more children. I accept that I didn't graduate college and pursue a career. I accept Your plan.

God's girl,
Molly

March 21, 2018

The sleep study was productive. They found out that I have central sleep apnea, and that I stop breathing for 39 seconds every half hour. When I heard that I kinda freaked out, and didn't want to try and sleep again. That's why I'm sooo tired and my memory has problems.

They're going to try and run more tests, but my insurance is being a bit wacky. I'm glad we at least have some answers and that the solution is more oxygen. But unfortunately, I have to always sleep with that weird tube in my nose.

I started being a big pain about that part, but then David told me that I could die if I don't use it. He said he didn't want to find me dead in bed one day, and that scared me a bit.

God's girl,
Molly

April 16, 2018

The lab sleep study came back better than the home sleep study. As of now, it shows that I have extremely minor central sleep apnea. While it is good news to have an answer, it means that my exhaustion and memory/mental acuity issues are still unanswered. I'm a little disappointed, but thankful to be alive.

God's girl,
Molly

❧ ❧

Looking back after all these years, I now realize David was pressuring me into thinking, because of my condition, I couldn't go to church on Sundays anymore. In deep wrestling with Jesus, I considered not going and adhering to David's request for me to stay home. He constantly pestered me with comments about how I was so exhausted from Monday to Wednesday because I went to church on Sundays. I didn't remember being tired, but then I didn't remember a lot of things that he said happened. He said I couldn't handle the loud noises. I prayed and asked God for wisdom. Finally, I submitted to David and said that I could not go to church.

I sent this to my pastors and the prayer team on April 19, 2018

> Alright, I'm sad to say this but I will no longer be a part of the prayer team. I get too overwhelmed by the sounds of people at church. I'm still praying for our congregation, but merely at home. I will not be attending church because I'm noise-sensitive, but will be at city group every week.
>
> I thought the sleep study would give me a drug to make my tiredness less, and help my memory be more intact, but they didn't. We're still going to the doctor to try and understand what I'm going through, but for now I'm not attending church on Sunday and only going to city group on Wednesdays where less people are around. I hope you understand this.

Later that morning

When I was younger, I made all these declarations about how I would give "anything and everything for Christ," or "to live is Christ and to die is gain," "count the cost for Jesus," and "all to Jesus I surrender."

It's funny because when I was younger, I thought I could do something to change the world; to transform people's lives by sharing the gospel with thousands of people. I thought I was going to have a great testimony of how I did amazing stuff. But God. Yeah, He had to act and you know, allow me that stroke at 20. Paralyzing me completely on my right side. Stuck in a coma.

But what if the cost for following Jesus is having a stroke? Heart surgery? A TIA? Sleep problems? Memory loss? Not driving? Church/big crowds being too noisy to handle? 9/10 signs of dementia? At 28.

What if I'm supposed to die a long death of forgetting my husband's name? At 28. What if I'm to surrender my memory? My short-term and long-term memory? What if it means I'm to surrender my hopes of seeing the world, traveling to Europe, living in a city with lots of people, having tons of people over?

I've talked with David often about how I don't want to get old. I want to be young and free of problems like Alzheimer's, cancer, ALS, heart attacks, and other dying diseases. But I'm 28 years old and have already suffered a lot of medical issues still ahead for many 60-year-olds.

I take peace in knowing God is loving, faithful, loyal, consistent, forever, holy, righteous, and gracious to me. Psalm 32:7 comforts me: "You are a hiding place for me; You preserve me from trouble; You surround me with shouts of deliverance."

I know that I'm going to mentally die before I physically die, and that scares me. I'm sad to be alone every day for most of the day because David works and Alex is in school. I am just here. I can't really talk other than between now and noon when I have the mental energy to say a few words.

I decided that I'm not going to church anymore—which was a big decision because I have served Christ's body since I was in 6th grade. I'm sad about that. It's like I'm grieving both church and my mother in-law.

God's girl,
Molly

October 2, 2018

Yesterday I called my parents and told them the following, and I cried as I told Jane. I also texted David's whole family and they all supported me.

> Hi everyone…I have good news and bad news. The good news is the doctor fixed my prescription for the medication that helped. He set it for a year, so I won't have an issue getting it anymore.
>
> The bad news is that I have early onset Alzheimer's. I cried last night, to say the least. The stroke I had eight years ago damaged my brain, especially my speech section. That damage has caused the Alzheimer's. The medication helps, but I don't know how long it will help. It could be a year or 45 years. I will start forgetting people, things, events.
>
> Know that I still care about you even when I can't remember your name, an event we went to, or some details of your life. I'm so thankful that I serve a God who knows every detail of my own life—Jesus who surrounds me with comfort as I weep. A friend reminded me that Jesus wept too. I will try to answer any questions you may have. I love you all.

October 9, 2018

God's peace fills my heart. I danced, sang, and raised my hands in my bedroom. I have some Christian artists on my playlist and I sang with them. So thankful to Jesus for being good, glorious, and gracious.

God's girl,
Molly

Why I Believe

I believe in Jesus,
some people ask why
I would put my life in His hand
instead of just crying and sigh.

The Lord has been good to me,
though my life is hard,
He has provided what I can see,
the ocean, mountain, and my backyard.

I believe He is good,
in creating color in the sky,
in allowing trees to form into wood,
In creating the birds and I.

He allowed me to speak again,
And move around my hand,
Walking without a cane
To faraway places and land.

Every day and everything,
He has provided for me-
food, water, shelter, and
All the goodness that I can see.

I trust that I am safe in His arms,
Whether I remember His grace,
Or forget my every need,
For one day I shall see His face.

He has said I am His and He is mine,
And I trust in His Word,
To rest forever in His mercy,
Even as my reconciliation blurred.

Through hardships great and small,
From paralyzed to forgetfulness,
He is with me through them all,
On His presence I have faith.

I cling to hope, faith, and love,
In Jesus I will sing,
As I lift up His name,
And let my voice rise and ring.

MGM Nov. '18

CHAPTER 12

Love Christ

As David no longer loved Christ, the Lord's love for me became even more real. I had always loved Christ, even when I was a young girl. Jesus loved me intimately and I began to fathom the extent of His perfect love for me. I re-read the poems I wrote when I was a teenager and I loved God even more now.

True Love

Romantic red roses and pretty pink hearts,
Arouse love this time of year,
Where our desire is for another soul,
As Valentine's Day grows near.

Yet, thoughts of true love may contradict,
Any painful experience from the past,
And tears may flow on Valentine's Day,
For regret can overtake the mind fast.

Our hearts may long for that 'special someone'
To affectionately bestow upon us hugs and kisses,
But my King's Intimate, Selfless Sacrifice Eternally Satisfies,
More than any person and fulfilled wishes.

He humbled Himself when He came here,
And willingly died in our place,
Yet He overcame death and is alive today,
Offering us His love and grace.

Love between man and wife is a wonderful treasure,
Where "till death do us part" is a promise made,
Which requires hard work and selfless sacrifices,
But Christ's love will survive beyond the grave your body fades.

He is patient, kind, and forgives as well,
Forever faithful He will be.
He understands life's many concerns,
And sincerely loves us farther than eyes can see.

Christ passionately loves you more than anyone ever can,
He always listens and knows you better too,
And He wants to remind you this Valentine's Day,
Of His sacrifice and true love for you.

-MG February '05

1 John 4:10, 11 NIV
This is love: not that we loved God, but that he loved us and sent his Son as an atoning sacrifice for our sins. Dear friends, since God so loved us, we also ought to love one another.

Romans 8:35, 37-39 NIV
Who shall separate us from the love of Christ? Shall trouble or hardship or persecution or famine or nakedness or danger or sword? No, in all these things we are more than conquerors through him who loved us. For I am convinced that neither death nor life, neither angels nor demons, neither the present nor the future, nor any powers, neither height nor depth, nor anything else in all creation, will be able to separate us from the love of God that is in Christ Jesus our Lord.

Only Your Love

Oh Jesus, how it hurts,
My heart is torn and breaking,
Free me from this pain,
As my body shivers from shaking.

I've given away my heart again,
Though You warned me to hold on,
I foolishly turned my ears from You,
Now I wonder when these tears will be gone.

Father, forgive me, I was wrong,
Help me gather every broken piece,
Take them all and make me whole,
Heal me, Jesus, make the pain cease.

I need You to be my strength,
I'm tired, weary, and broken,
Please heal my wounds and be my shield,
Calming me with Words You've spoken.

Only Your love makes me complete,
Your passionate, intimate love,
Through seasons of pain You remain,
Showering Your strength from above.

Be my refuge in times of weakness,
When I'm tempted to stray once more,
Hold me close in Your strong Arms,
I'm trusting You like never before.

Oh Jesus, help me let go,
Surrendering everything to You,
Remembering only Your love,
Here are the pieces, please make me new.
-MG January '06

Psalm 13:5 NIV
But I trust in your unfailing love; my heart rejoices in your salvation.

Psalm 147:3 NIV
He heals the brokenhearted and binds up their wounds.

2 Corinthians 1:3, 4 NIV
Praise be to the God and Father of our Lord Jesus Christ, the Father of compassion and the God of all comfort, who comforts us in all our troubles, so that we can comfort those in any trouble with the comfort we ourselves receive from God.

Hosea 2:14,16, 19, 20 NIV
Therefore, behold, I will allure her, and bring her into the wilderness, and speak tenderly to her. "And in that day," declares the Lord, "you will call Me 'My Husband,' and no longer will you call Me 'My Baal.' And I will betroth you to Me forever. I will betroth you to Me in righteousness and in justice, in steadfast love and in mercy. I will betroth you to Me in faithfulness. And you shall know the Lord."

The Lord is "My Husband." I told David that Jesus was my husband when David refused to sleep with me. He's distancing himself from me more and more now.

December 1, 2018

Sadly, I cannot cook anymore. This past week I have forgotten the stove was on, left the kettle on for way too long, forgotten to turn the oven off, set a pot on fire, and snapped at Alex while cooking. David told me I cannot cook anymore. I'm bummed, but I knew it was going to happen. Most people who have Alzheimer's get burned, set on fire or badly hurt in the kitchen. David is preparing for that to happen.

I know he means well. He's not working now and we will figure out meal-prepping ahead of time. David is taking December off of work, and then in January he will do a six-month study course to become a software engineer. We're not sure which health benefits we'll use yet—but it will be some kind of insurance because of me. I pray that we'll be okay.

Dear Lord, here I am. I'm Yours. Thank You for being faithful, honest, loving, kind, and gracious. I praise You for Your goodness, mercy, and love. Thank You that You are here with me now. Please help me. Help me to be gentle with David and Alex.

Forgive my jealousy of David's friends that they get to experience things I can't experience. Forgive my conceit and selfish ambitions. Forgive my bickering, shortness, and impatience. Help me be kind to everyone. Help me be gentle in my speech and take time to listen. Help me not get overwhelmed by people talking.

Help me not to yell at David, which I apparently did in the middle of the night, although I don't remember. Help me to always remember Your forgiveness and compassion. Help me to be Your hands and feet even when I'm alone in my room. Help me to pray for people and for You to answer my prayers. Be glorified through me. Be magnified. Be magnificent. Be the true King of Kings and Lord of Lords. I love You Lord. Thank You for Your love. In Jesus' name, amen.

God's girl,
Molly

December 4, 2019

Dear Jesus, thank You that my neurologist is testing my brain for an hour today. Thank You that You gave me Your peace last night as my friend prayed over me. I felt the burden lift off of me as she prayed for God's peace to fill my heart and mind and body. We'll hear back from them on my birthday!

God's girl,
Molly

December 5, 2019

Thank You dear Father for all the people who care about me and are praying with me regarding my neurologist testing and my neuropsychology testing in January. Thank You for the body of Believers that extends to almost every continent. Thank You that Alex and I just read this morning about the new earth and the new heaven. Thank You that we will never cry there, nor will there be any mourning or pain. I'm very excited about that because I'm in pain right now and I'm still mourning Mom Mulano. Thank You that I will be healed from my stroke, my heart tumor, my Alzheimer's, and my loads of other issues. Thank You that You are my Healer and my Redeemer. Thank You that You, Jesus, died on the cross for my sins. Thank You that You rose from the dead conquering my sins. Thank You that You are alive in Heaven waiting for me. Thank You that You sent Your Holy Spirit of truth and sanctification to me. Thank You that You help me always.

God's girl,
Molly

January 3, 2020

Yesterday, David drove me to my appointment. It lasted from 7:45 am until 2:15 pm. We started by telling the doctor everything that has happened to me medically since my stroke. The doctor said something cool about my brain being like a grapefruit, and the stroke scraped the peel off of the left side of my brain. As a result, the left side of my brain has not been able to get the "thoughts" to my memory section.

I also learned that David has taken caffeine away from me for the past two years—including caffeinated coffee and tea. I've been drinking decaf coffee and tea for two years and they've had a placebo effect on me. Apparently, David has told me this again and again, but I don't remember it. The doctor also made me feel that it's okay to be sad. My life has changed so drastically—not just since the stroke, but over the past year—and feeling sad is normal.

They did a test similar to the MoCA test, but on steroids. They did the "normal" stuff—like having me draw a clock, draw a triangle thing, say 'cow' when a cow was drawn, or 'boat' when I saw a boat. They had me match letters to numbers. Many of the tests involved repeating words and having me remember them. That one was tricky for me.

I also got confused during the second section of my tests. I failed a lot. But that's okay. My brain just can't handle all the words.

I wish the Lord would just tell me ahead of time what will happen. Oh, I wish the Lord would "fix" me! Oh, I wish and pray that the Lord would heal me of all my horrible sicknesses and diagnoses. *I'm tired, Lord, I'm so tired. Please help me.*

After hearing a song about praising Jesus, I wrote:

Yes, Lord. Your will be done—not mine—Yours. Your life be glorified—not mine—Yours. You should receive all the praise. All the glory. All the honor. Help me lead others to You. Help my life be the one who points more people to You.

You, Jesus, are great and good. You who have suffered so much that I am forgiven, accepted, redeemed, and made whole. You, who died on the cross for my sins. Because of me. I did that. I wanted my way, not Your way. I wanted, and You received the nails. You bore the burden and took the penalty for my sins. I did that to You. I nailed You to the cross. The agony You must have felt. The pain You endured. The suffering You unjustly experienced for my sake.

Thank You. I praise You. May Your will be done in my circumstances. I don't know what is going on in my body. But You know precisely what, why, and how because You designed me. Please help me to feel better. Please make Your name be known through all of this. May at least one person know You as their Savior through my suffering. Please, Lord.

God's girl,
Molly

1 John 2:2 NIV
He is the atoning sacrifice for our sins, and not only for ours but also for the sins of the whole world.

Ephesians 3:18, 19 NIV
…may have power, together with all the saints, to grasp how wide and long and high and deep is the love of Christ, and to know this love that surpasses knowledge—that you may be filled to the measure of all the fullness of God.

Colossians 2:10 New King James Version (NKJV)
…and you are complete in Him…

Philippians 3:8 NIV
What is more, I consider everything a loss because of the surpassing worth of knowing Christ Jesus my Lord, for whose sake I have lost all things. I consider them garbage, that I may gain Christ….

Heart's Desire

By whom and what do we identify?
Fame, fortune, family and friends,
Is that what we often clarify,
As a successful life, lived well to the end?

Popular, accepted, and liked by all,
Is how we'd love to be seen,
Yet, even if we're respected by most,
Will the days to come sparkle and gleam?

What if we buy fashionable clothes,
For we want society to be impressed,
Or what if we drive stylish cars,
Will our hearts then be at rest?

Possessions from this world may attract,
But will it ever be enough?
Enjoyment may be momentary,
And after all, isn't it just stuff?

Maybe sports consume our time,
Or maybe drama's our preferred taste,
But do our activities really define who we are,
Or in the end will it all be a waste?

If we perfect every technique,
And with effort try all day long,
To be the best that we can be,
Will our need for more be prolonged?

Maybe if someone is truly interested in us,
Actually cherishes, adores, and admires,
Would we be completed with romance,
Or deep inside do we have a greater desire?

No matter how hard we attempt,
To cram our days with pleasure,
We still won't be satisfied,
Despite the season and weather.

Something is missing in our hearts,
There's a void we cannot fill,
We keep searching for the answer,
Searching with all our might and will.

Yet, we need not look any farther,
For the Maker of the world, yes, He,
Chose us before He formed the earth,
And loves us deeper than the sea.

Our true identity is in Him alone,
For His amazing love will never dim,
And we can now fulfill our created purpose,
That is, a relationship with Him.

Christ shed His blood for thee,
But painful death was not defeat,
For His sacrifice restores our souls,
And in Him we become complete.

-MG February '05

Chapter 13

Rejoice in Jesus

What is joy? Is it happiness? Is it contentment? What does Paul mean in Philippians 4:4 to "Rejoice in Christ?" I struggled with being happy in life. Even before I had my stroke, I just didn't see the point of being joyful. I was always so serious, except at home with my sister and parents. We laughed a lot growing up. Yet, true joy is something more than laughing occasionally.

Never before could I say I rejoiced in anything, holding my brand-new son brought me so much joy! As Alex got bigger and bigger, the joy of playing with him also grew. Having a son brought me some happiness, but also joy grew deep inside of me.

I could understand why, throughout Scripture, such as Psalm 21:6; 43:4; and Habakkuk 3:17, 18, we are called to rejoice in knowing our Lord. How? Personally. Redeeming. Saving. Intimately. Passionately.

In our trials, James 1:2, 3 calls us to "count it all joy." Philippians is a book full of joy and rejoicing in Jesus. And you know who wrote the letter? Paul, while he was imprisoned!

Here was I, struggling with my memory in Jesus-friendly country, whereas Paul was captive because of what he said about Jesus. And, in Philippians 1:18, he rejoiced in Jesus, knowing that the gospel was going forth and proclaimed while he was in jail.

The world does not revolve around me. Nor does it revolve around you. I needed that reminder. So often I would compare my life to someone else's—someone who looked happy. Yet, Jesus commanded us to have joy, not compare our lives to theirs.

Below are a few collected past and present journal entries that talk about joy

January 1, 2013

Happy New Year!

I have finally figured out why God gave me Alex as a gift, a son who has almost grown out of two-year-old clothes and he's not two till March...a son who talks more than I do...a son who is nearly as strong as I am...a son who is loud and rambunctious...a son who likes sharing with others...a son who plays well with adults...a son who is up earlier and goes to bed early...a son who yells hello to every person on the street...all of these wonderful things were given to me so that I will never be bored. Alex is a handful, and I'm glad our Father holds and loves us both so tightly. I love Alex but God loves him even more than I do.

God's girl,
Molly

February 9, 2013

We're visiting David's family in Texas. *Oh Lord, please help me calm down and relax.* Alex woke everyone up at 4am, but thankfully the Mulano family went back to sleep. I, however, am still up with him.

Lord, I'm tired and still a little bit angry. Help me let go of my frustration regarding David—that he doesn't change Alex's diapers and that he sleeps through Alex's crying. Thank You that Alex is getting older and going to potty train soon. Thank You that You are God who shows me Your compassion, kindness, grace, and love. Help me do the same with David and Alex. Thank You that You are Lord of my life...so here's my heart, mind, soul, hands, spirit, and everything else. Help me surrender every moment of every day.

God's girl,
Molly

February 23, 2015

Ephesians 6:1-3 (the first commandment with a promise):
"Children, obey your parents in the Lord, for this is right. Honor your father and mother that it may go well with you and that you may live long in the land."
Proverbs 6:20
"My son, keep your father's commandment, and forsake not your mother's teaching."

Why, Lord, do you not give me a more direct form for disciplining Alex? Thank You for giving me the joy of Alex.

God's girl,
Molly

Below are a few of my posts on Facebook as I responded to my latest diagnosis

May 9, 2019

The Lord's plans are not my plans. I reminded the people at our city group that and the Lord is reminding me again. Here He raised up the Chaldeans, "that bitter and hasty nation" to overtake the nation of Israel. Habakkuk was praying for the Lord's help, begging Him actually. God replied in Habakkuk 1:5: "Look among the nations, and see; wonder and be astounded. For I am doing a work in your days that you would not believe if I told you."

And that statement gets me excited—like wow, here God is going to do something big, amazing, and glorifying... and yet His plans are so not my plans. Here I am, a 29-year-old girl having suffered a stroke at 20 while on my honeymoon, had open heart surgery, a TIA, and currently living with Alzheimer's while trying to parent my 8-year-old child. Do you think I would have planned this? No way. But God allowed it. He knew before I was born all that would happen to me. And here I am. Sometimes I get bitter that these things happened to me and I wish that they didn't. But other times, I accept them and live with my faith in my Faithful Jesus. "Behold, his soul is puffed up; it is not upright within him, but the righteous shall live by his faith" (Habakkuk 2:4).

Though we do not have a lot of money, I echo his statement of faith in Habakkuk 3:17-19 and do truly take joy in my LORD:

> Though the fig tree should not blossom,
> nor fruit be on the vines,
> the produce of the olive fail
> and the fields yield no food,
> the flock be cut off from the fold
> and there be no herd in the stalls,
> yet I will rejoice in the LORD;
> I will take joy in the God of my salvation.
> GOD, the Lord, is my strength;
> he makes my feet like the deer's;
> he makes me tread on my high places.

December 6, 2018

Happiness is not my main goal in life—it never has been. As God's girl, I am called to rejoice in Christ, but that doesn't mean I will always be "happy." Rejoicing in Christ means choosing joy because of Jesus. It means hoping in Jesus. It means making myself merry because of Jesus. According to Psalm 31:7, "I will rejoice and be glad in Your steadfast love, because You have seen my affliction; You have known the distress of my soul."

I choose joy because of the Lord's love for me. I choose joy because He has seen my affliction. I choose joy because of Jesus. Because He suffered so much for me. Because He was beaten, jeered, and mocked. Because He chose to not be with the Father and be utterly alone. Because He died on the cross for me. Because He rose again for me.

I rejoice in Jesus because of who He is:

My Shepherd who takes care of me, His sheep.
My Refuge when life rains all its worst on me.
My Healer for one day I will be in His presence completely healed.
My Forgiver for He has erased all my sins.
My Redeemer who has redeemed me.
My Hope for I hope in Him.
My Faithful Friend who will never leave me nor forsake me.
My All-powerful, All-present, All-knowing God.
My Creator who created the skies, the mountains, and the birds.
My Designer who knows every hair on my head and every breath that I breathe.
My Giver who gives me all things.
My Provider who provides for me.
My Lover who passionately, intimately loves me.

My Prince of peace who sacrificed Himself for me.
My Savior who died for me and rose again.
My Shelter who keeps me close in His arms.

I rejoice in Christ because of that. Sometimes at night I go through the A-B-Cs naming who He is—Amazing, Bold, Creator—and that helps me fall asleep. Other nights I toss and turn, unable to be still and sleep. I listen to podcasts, sermons, and the reading of Scripture to put me to sleep along with 150 mg of a drug that they say 50 mg of would knock out a huge football player for three days. But I'm not a football player, I am…

God's girl.
Molly

February 23, 2020

The joy of my son is so thrilling at times! He brings me so much joy and gladness. I pray for the women who don't have children of their own because of infertility. I pray for the women who have carried a baby, but that baby doesn't live to be born. I pray for the lostness, loneliness, heart ache, pain, and waiting. I pray for you all to have children who want children, but also that you may find joy in the Lord.

God's girl,
Molly

August 11, 2020

This morning I saw the most beautiful sunrise. Then Alex and I read through Proverbs 8 where it talks about wisdom. We talked about wisdom, what it is/is not, and how Jesus is Wisdom. We read through The Passion Translation because it is easier for Alex to understand. I love verse 30, "I was there, close to the Creator's side as His master artist. Daily He was filled with delight in me as I playfully rejoiced before Him."

I've been thinking and mediating on how magnificent God is as the artist of our lives. He designed and painted the sky this morning. I captured on my camera Alex and me playing with his stuffed animals today. And then I thought about how this verse describes my relationship with my child. He painted Alex to be a part of my life. He painted the whining days of him as a four-year-old. He painted the laughter of both of us. Daily, He filled me with delight in Him because of my son. I did not rejoice often before Alex was born. Before Alex, I had a difficult season of my stroke and countless friends going through rough times. Then Alex came and I was "filled with delight.

I rejoiced that Jesus counted me worthy enough to give me a son. I rejoiced in Jesus that He counted me worthy enough to rescue me from my sin. I rejoiced in Jesus even when the days were very long and hard. If you have a child, you know the cost of parenthood. If you don't or can't have a child and want one, I weep for you. I pray for you often that the Lord will teach you the lesson of joy through another means.

God's Girl,
Molly

CHAPTER 14

Intercession

As I prayed about what God wanted me to do at home alone a lot, prayer kept coming to my attention. I had always loved talking with Jesus and began to pray more.

God called me to pray for myself, but also for family, friends, strangers, people I just met, missionaries, and those overseas. All people need prayer just as much as you do—whether they are working the cash register or at the gas station or the homeless person on the street or co-workers or moms with strollers.

Psalms are full of prayers and merely talking to the Father, which is the definition of prayer. Intercession is praying for somebody else. In Scripture we find both Jesus (Hebrews 7:25 and Romans 8:34) and the Holy Spirit (Romans 8:26, 27) interceding for us. I find it a great comfort that the Holy Spirit prays.

I challenge you to pray for yourself but also to intercede and pray for someone else. If only for five or ten minutes a day. Write a list of people you meet who need prayer. Pray consistently and persistently. While you're washing dishes, pray for someone. If you don't know what to pray, pray certain Bible verses for someone else. Place your name and someone else's name in Ephesians 1:15-23; 3:14-21; 6:10-20; Colossians 1:9-14; James 5:13-18 and John 17:1-26.

Matthew 9:37, 38 urges us to pray for people to become Christians and for more to labor to make that happen. "Then He [Jesus] said to his disciples, 'The harvest is plentiful, but the laborers are few; therefore pray earnestly to the Lord of the harvest to send out laborers into his harvest.'"

Pray and watch God do amazing things. Sometimes He immediately answers my prayers, but other times I never see the benefit of that specific prayer. Sometimes He says No and other times Wait. Don't give up hope and stop praying just because your life is not how you would like it to be, or the person you're praying for still doesn't love Jesus. Throughout the Scriptures, we are commanded to pray on our own and to pray together as a group of intercessors.

In regards to prayer, I read many books by *Voice of the Martyrs* (VOM) and discovered *Open Doors,* which is now called *Global Christian Relief.* The first time I ever heard of VOM it was through a book titled *Jesus Freaks* by DC Talk. In 6th grade, I remember reading the book and being encouraged by stories of faith of persecuted believers. Years later, I began to intercede for persecuted Christians around the globe.

Global Christian Relief is another prayer partner for the persecuted believers. I too am persecuted for my faith because David no longer believes in Jesus. He verbally yells at me for my faith, but there are people who are brutally killed for merely saying the name of Jesus. There are people who need prayer in Afghanistan and North Korea that are persecuted far more than me.

So, I prayed for them. I interceded for those who desperately need the One who is in control. I downloaded two apps on my phone: Global Christian Relief and VOM. I would encourage you to, as well. Intercede for those who need intercession.

Pray without Ceasing

Pray without Ceasing,
Is what You ask of me.
Always keep praying,
Is what You desire, I see.

Ask You to give me more
Of Yourself to me and
Of myself to You, Lord!
Help me to give to Your Hand.

Help me to give You all;
Everything inside of me,
The good and the bad fall
Into Your Hand to be.

Lord, I give You all
Of my passionate devotion,
Of my thoughts, big and small,
Of my inaction and action.

I plead for the homeless,
As I see them on the street,
And for those that are childless,
As we whimper and weep.

I plead for the nations
As I'm putting my dishes away,
For all of the train stations,
As I walk throughout the day.

I plead for the children, yes,
In this persecuted world,
They'd meet Jesus, nonetheless,
That their universe would twirl.

I plead for the movie stars
On TV, as I watch them,
And those behind the bars,
For Jesus to forgive, not condemn.

I plead for the Church,
brothers and sisters, Persecuted.
Around the globe as they're searched,
They're mocked and they're executed.

I plead for my church too,
That the love of Christ would
Compel us to live with You,
That we would praise Jesus as good.

Thankful that God listens,
To every cry and prayer.
The Holy Spirit's Mission
Is to pray and to always care.
-MGM December '19

Romans 12:12
Rejoice in hope, be patient in tribulation, be constant in prayer.

Ephesians 6:18
…praying at all times in the Spirit, with all prayer and supplication. To that end, keep alert with all perseverance, making supplications for all the saints.

Colossians 4:2
Continue steadfastly in prayer, being watchful in it with thanksgiving.

1 Thessalonians 5:17
Pray without ceasing…

Luke 11:9
And I tell you, ask, and it will be given to you; seek, and you will find; knock, and it will be opened to you.

☙ ❧

November 2019

My Pastor anointed me with oil according to James 5:14, 15 and prayed for God's healing. Pastor Jim and my city group prayed over me that God would take away my Alzheimer's. The woman who leads my city group said she clearly felt the Spirit's power as they prayed.

For whatever reason, the Lord did not heal me completely. I feel like Paul, begging God for healing over and over again in 2 Corinthians 12. Yet, God did not heal Paul, the apostle who even a handkerchief that touched him healed other people (Acts 19:11, 12).

Second Corinthians 12:7-10 says of Paul regarding his ailment:

> So to keep me from becoming conceited because of the surpassing greatness of the revelations, a thorn was given me in the flesh, a messenger of Satan to harass me, to keep me from becoming conceited. Three times I pleaded with the Lord about this, that it should leave me. But He said to me, "My grace is sufficient for you, for My power is made perfect in weakness." Therefore I will boast all the more gladly of my weaknesses, so that the power of Christ may rest upon me. For the sake of Christ, then, I am content with weaknesses, insults, hardships, persecutions, and calamities. For when I am weak, then I am strong.

I felt like Paul, and was reassured by this passage. God's grace is sufficient for me. I can do Alzheimer's because Jesus' strength is made perfect in my weakness.

God's girl,

Molly

March 2, 2020

Well, I haven't been journaling because I've had to hand write my prayer every morning for my discipleship group. It's 1 o'clock in the afternoon and a lot of thoughts have been racing through my mind and I figured I needed to journal.

Dear Lord, here I am with a thousand thoughts racing through my brain. Where to start? First here's a text message that I sent to my friend Amy:

I guess I need to write about my conversation with David and his friends. So often I apologize to them for whatever sin I have committed against them, or something that I have to apologize for. Time and time again.

So anyhow, dear Lord, thank You for reminding me I too have sinned against them and needed to confess and repent. Thank You for taking that sin and nailing it to the cross. Thank You that You forgive me, even if she, let's call her Sandy, doesn't forgive me. Thank You that You are enough for me, that You love me entirely. Thank You for Your intimate, passionate love, which I haven't felt from David. For the past year and a half, David hasn't loved me sexually because he says he's too tired and unable. You used that time to draw me closer to Yourself, to show me that You love me completely. I remember the poems I wrote as an 8th grader proclaiming how much You loved me. You still unfailingly love me. Thank You. Please help me need You, not the intimacy I crave with David. I need You. Please help me stay in Your love. In Jesus' name, amen.

God's Girl,

Molly

Later that day

On another note, eleven people loved my written prayer for China on Facebook and two people said "Amen." I didn't really know what to think of it. A lot of people have liked/loved my prayers for the persecuted people and that's taken me aback. I don't write those prayers to get people to "like" my prayer but to be heard by God regarding my prayer.

I think I'm used to going alone, living by myself and being the person of prayer. I believe in Jesus, but David and his friends do not. Alex is a child and so I teach him about Jesus. I try every morning as we get out our Bibles and I read a passage and we talk about what it means for his life.

So often I lead, and I forget when someone wants to serve me. I don't like it. Amy, and friends from church, often serve me or try to, but I push them away and feel like I'm strong enough to do things on my own. However, we as the body of Christ need each other.

On Friday I fasted and prayed for the salvation of my loved ones, and so many friend's family members. I prayed and prayed and prayed. It was a wonderful day filled with intercession.

We as a church fasted twice. I wasn't sure if I could fast because I wondered if the lack of food would cause me harm. I decided I would try. I didn't eat breakfast, snacks, and lunch. I craved food but I prayed that I would crave Jesus more. Jesus became more real, and He gave me words of intercession for the persecuted church, our church, my city group, and so much more.

I was on a group text with three other ladies who also fasted. We interceded for each other and shared our desires to consume food. And yet we didn't until Tuesday night when we broke our fast with bread and wine, symbolizing Jesus' body and blood. It was wonderful.

So, the next week I did it again for our church. Again, the Lord sustained me. Then Liz and I prayed for the persecuted church on Thursday like we always do. The salvation of our loved ones was also something we prayed over. The Lord really convinced me that people desperately need Him.

That Friday, Fatima and I talked about her fasting for Ramadan and how they can eat when the sun is down but not when the sun is up in April. We had agreed that morning to hang out at the park with our children after school.

I had already eaten breakfast at like 4:30 am and while I was walking to Walgreens my stomach growled. I thought about Fatima's fasting, and I decided that I would fast that day for her salvation and the salvation of so many other people. I didn't eat a snack or lunch and waited till dinner. I interceded for sooo many people while I fasted, and I felt so close to Jesus.

God's girl,
Molly

March 8, 2020

I woke up Saturday morning feeling like crap. I knew I would, and I prayed to withstand the enemy's attacks after I fasted. I was very worn down, weary, and did not have strength to endure.

Then I received a text from Kari that took me by surprise but was what I needed at that very moment:

> "David was now in great danger. But David found strength in the Lord his God."
>
> *1 Samuel 30:6 The Living Translation (TLT)*

I replied "Amen—I need that strength today."

And then she replied:

"Lord Jesus, thank You for knowing exactly what Your children need and exactly how to provide for those needs. Strengthen my sister in Your Spirit today. Encourage her and breathe life into her weariness. Thank you that You are the lifter of her head. Help her to rest in all Your promises for her and to be still and know that YOU ARE GOD. We love You, in Your name we pray."

At that point I was blown away by my amazing God's love for me, that He knew I had no strength of my own and yet He PROVIDED me with the strength through Kari. He knew I needed encouragement to sustain my weariness and He gave me more than enough.

❧ ☙

March 9, 2020

So often I get weary because I don't get to see the fruit of my prayers. I want to be doing service, I always have wanted to seek out how I can serve Christ. Everything has been taken away from me, except prayer, painting, and reading. "Taken away" is how I view it, but my husband would say it's for my own safety. I believe him. I asked God what He wants me to do, and "prayer" came to mind. I asked again, and He replied "Pray." So I prayed.

The body of Christ is still working in Texas and around the globe. As part of "The Body" each part must do its work, as I have read thousands of times. In city group someone pointed out that the Body of Christ isn't a "hand" all by itself. It needs the foot and the heart and the intestines to function as the body.

I thought about that a lot. I often think "I'm all they need" referring to "lesser" Christians. Such pride! I can go too far and think the Christians who are persecuted "need" my prayers of intercession. Just like God told me when I was hospitalized from the stroke, they don't "need" me, but they need Him and He will work it all out according to His plan. He reminded me yesterday through Kari's texted prayer that we are all the body of Christ. As Christians, we need each other to survive and thrive.

God's girl,
Molly

March 11, 2020

David and I just had a really good conversation. We both cried. A lot. He asked me to stop accusing him of not caring. For the past seven years, he has cared for me and has taken on the burden of being my husband. He is emotionally spent.

My fear of him being the man I passionately fell in love with sleeping with other women is a false fear according to him. He has nothing left, including his emotions. He is not the passionate man he was seven years ago. He is done pretending to be the sacrificial and loving husband that men of God told him to be.

He has loved me for 20 years. The past four years, he has cared for me so much. He does not at all want to divorce me but wants to care for me "till death do us part." He's done pretending to be a "Thomas Kincade" painting because he has no energy from lack of sleep from taking care of me. He has no emotions from trying to survive.

He's done answering questions, and a hundred times "how are you" because he's tired the same way he was six years ago. He can sleep for a week or four weeks and be "energized" but it doesn't change how I am doing. He's taken care of me, and cleaned up the house, put me to bed, put Alex to bed, and been alone at night for years.

His sex drive is gone, his dopamine is gone, his testosterone is gone. He needs me to not ask him questions about him or me or what I need, but for me to text others what I need, and my needs will be met. He needs me to love him by not wanting perfection, thinking it will be enough if he does this. He needs me to love him by spending time with him and not talking but reading near him.

He wants me to love him by accepting that I have dementia and that it's not getting any better. I need to accept that my memory is fading. I need to accept that I had a stroke and am not getting back April 17, 2010 for the 7 hours we were married before I had the stroke.

I need to not bring up Jesus but pray for him. I need to let him be himself by being with his friends. He claims he hasn't slept sexually with anyone but me. And I need to accept that and not accuse him of sleeping around. He hasn't written me a letter because he gets to the first sentence, and he doesn't have anything to say or write.

He is not some romantic man who whisks me off my feet anymore. He loved me and wrote me love letters before I had the stroke. He has kept me alive and worked so hard at living. He has thought hard and tried to find a way to die but leave Alex and me with three million dollars. I cried and said I don't want that money. I love him way too much to want him to die.

So now I wait and try to accept being forgetful. Try to accept that David doesn't "need" me, that he has two girlfriends (who he claims are just there to help him).

God's girl,
Molly

❧ ❧

My Facebook entries when the COVID Shutdown began

March 13, 2020

To those affected by Corona virus/ COVID-19 virus as Christians, do not fear for the LORD your God will help you (Isaiah 41:13). We are taking precautions with Clorox/hand sanitizer/gloves, and I hope you are too so that we can prevent the virus from spreading.

But I want to remind you that God is a God of order not chaos (1 Corinthians 14:33). Remember to pray (1 Thessalonians 5:17). Don't allow all the anxieties of this virus to weigh you down but take ALL of your requests to the Lord and remember HE IS WITH YOU (Philippians 4:5-7).

My heart is at peace because I know my days are numbered (Psalm 39:4, 5; 139:16). I'm not afraid to die (Philippians 1:21). To those of you who do not share our faith in Jesus our Savior, please consider what will happen to you if you die (Romans 3:23). Ask other Christians. We'll tell you all about Jesus' sacrifice on the cross for our sins (Ephesians 2:4-10). We'll tell you about how He rose from the dead and what that means to us (Acts 2:24-41).

God's girl,
Molly

March 15, 2020

As I was walking around here and the scenery was so quiet, I thought about the people who would normally be going to church. If that's you, do not fear for the Lord our God is with you. This morning I read a Psalm and thanked God for his faithfulness. He is with me even though I'm quarantined from the virus. He is with me even though I haven't been able to go to church now for nearly two years.

I would encourage all of you to listen to music by either Chris Tomlin or Matt Redman. If you can't meet in person, set up a Skype/FaceTime/Duo meeting like I'm doing with my discipleship group.

If you have kids, be creative and maybe follow along with some structure or daily schedule. If you have money to spend, give generously to those who do not have money to spare.

And remember Isaiah 41:10:

> Fear not, for I am with you; be not dismayed, for I am your God; I will strengthen you; I will help you, I will uphold you with My righteous right hand.

God's girl,
Molly

March 18, 2020

Is anyone else out there scared? I admit that I'm not afraid of personally dying but I do fear David and Alex's deaths. And the unknown. I constantly must lay that fear down at the cross. I pray for God to provide for the people who do not have money. I'm praying for our church and the Church worldwide to be Jesus' hands and help out those in need.

I think of Jesus dying for our sins. He actually sweated blood and prayed that God would take this cup from Him, but not as He wants but God's will be done (Luke 22:39-46). The fact that he "sweat blood" means something. Do you "sweat blood" when you're happy and everything is going well and wonderful?

No! He was crying out to His Father! It was a scary time and maybe He felt anxious about it but He was perfect and never sinned. How is that? Does that verse mean it's ok to be nervous but still trust God? I don't know. I hope so. That's where I'm at, nervous but still trusting God to know best.

God's girl,
Molly

March 20, 2020

I so miss Alex but I'm thankful he's with his friends. We quarantined ourselves because I'm "at risk." I've been without Alex for a week and have another week to go. We "Duo" called each other and also chatted with my Dad in San Diego. Additionally, we rescheduled my sleep doctor and neurologist appointments. I guess it's not God's timing for me to figure out why I'm not sleeping.

For my discipleship group, this week's memory verses are in Joshua 1:8, 9. Oh, what a powerful reminder to not to be frightened:

"This Book of the Law shall not depart from your mouth, but you shall meditate on it day and night, so that you may be careful to do according to all that is written in it. For then you will make your way prosperous, and then you will have good success. Have I not commanded you? Be strong and courageous. Do not be frightened, and do not be dismayed, for the LORD your God is with you wherever you go."

God's girl,
Molly

Journal entry

March 25, 2020

Dear Lord, You are sovereign, in control, and in charge of this situation. Thank You that I can trust You with everything. Thank You that I can bring all of my worries and fears. Thank You that I can lay them all down at the foot of the cross. Lord, I'm worried about Alex because people at the house got sick with a fever. This Coronavirus has everyone worried.

We're taking precautions like washing our hands for at least 20 seconds/Cloroxing everything/hand sanitizer/gloves for me. We're staying inside. David thought it wise if Alex stayed two extra weeks with his friends because he could have gotten the virus.

You know that Alex getting sick and dying has been one of my fears since he was born. You also know that I'm afraid of David dying. And they both could die. I don't know what the future holds. I can't count the stars or make everything in my life easy. I can't, but You can. You numbered the stars. You work everything out for Your good and glory. Thank You.

Thank You that I can trust You. Help me to trust You. Help Alex and David to trust You. Take care of my baby for me. Lord, I prayed last night for so long begging You to "move mountains" so to speak. I'm worn out.

Thank You that You know every detail of all the situations on earth. Thank You that You see all and care for all. Thank You for giving me lots of opportunities to speak Your Truth in love to countless other people. Thank You for the church service that was live streamed, and I got to be part of that.

Please continue to speak and teach me more about You. Please continue to pour out Your mercy to countless people, especially those in the medical field. Help them to come up with a cure. Help them, Lord. In Jesus' name, amen.

> The LORD Yahweh, commander of Angel Armies, makes this solemn decree: "Be sure of this: Just as I have planned, so it will be. Every purpose of my heart will surely come to pass.... For the Lord Yahweh, the commander of Angel Armies, has an amazing strategy, and who can thwart Him? When He moves in power, who can stop Him?" *Isaiah 14:24, 27 TPT*

Here in Isaiah, God is talking about His plan for the country of Assyria, but I think it applies to our situation with the virus. He knew it would happen. He knew people would lose their jobs being stuck inside quarantined. He knew Alex would get stuck at his friend's house. He knew every detail of every plan man makes and yet His plan is going to happen. His will WILL happen. Somehow, this is working out according to His plan.

God's girl,
Molly

Chapter 15

The COVID Nightmare

The first time David yelled at me was when we stayed overnight again in La Jolla in 2010. I was pregnant and had forgotten my anti-nausea medication, which I mentioned to David as we were driving there. He held his breath and glared at me intensely. His mood totally changed. It was like the man I married changed into a very angry person.

He told me how thoughtless I had been and how we didn't have the money to turn around, raising his voice. I automatically apologized over and over again. He said he forgave me and kept on driving there. I thought in my head that David had never been that angry with me.

I thought about how stupid I had been to forget my medication. I was so nervous and anxious about myself. I threw up a ton because I was nauseous from my pregnancy, and I was scared for the first time being married to David.

Suddenly, on the same day, David changed back into that nice, generous man I had married. But I couldn't just change like that! I wanted to talk it through with David, but he refused to go over it again. I had this knot in the pit of my stomach that wouldn't go away for three days.

That was the first of many arguments, disagreements, lies, and manipulations I went through. Ten, eleven years by his side. I realize now that he mentally, verbally, and psychologically abused me over those eleven years. He never hit me nor struck me. Physically, I was not abused. His words, though, twisted my thinking so I actually said out loud, "I'm bad, David is right, and he's unloved by me for selfishly doing x, y, z. I didn't respect him. I didn't acknowledge him."

He was still very popular and well-liked by others. Apparently, he took off his wedding ring for 6/7 years while we lived in Dallas and while I was at home with our son. He traveled a lot with the company, but I don't know where he went nor how much money he spent or with whom he slept.

Years later, I found out that he would buy drinks for people at the bars he frequented. He paid for rounds time and time again. Thousands of dollars he spent, while I was only allowed $80 every two weeks for groceries and living expenses for the three of us. From the time we were living in Chicago to Dallas that was my budget.

And man, in Chicago the groceries were expensive! Alex was a baby, so I had to get diapers too. All for under $80. Amy called it "Jesus math" because the Lord always provided. When we lived in the actual house in Dallas, I was given more money, but not a lot.

I asked permission for buying shoes and buying presents for our family. Sometimes he said yes, and other times I had to just give my nieces, nephew, and siblings gifts that I made. My family and other people bought me art supplies so I could paint.

He not only brought me down with words, but he also emotionally tested me. I hid the arguments and excused David's numerous mental breakdowns. I had to—that's what a self-sacrificing, Christian wife does. Or so I thought.

As soon as COVID hit, David got scared out of his mind. He controlled everything I did and the box he put me in got smaller and smaller. I was very depressed as I thought about my life. I prayed a ton for other people and for myself. I asked God why He allowed me to love cooking and then David took that away too.

I was sleeping irregularly—sometimes three hours a night, sometimes five. The hours I slept were broken up, with me waking up around two to seven times. David told me, demanded that I go to bed at 7pm and stop watching TV. I listened and obeyed. But that turned into David having friends over and me being placed aside. Out of sight, out of mind. I begged him to let me stay up later and he refused. He would get angry if I kept bringing it up.

I still loved him and desired to honor David. He was kind to me, fed me, clothed me, and provided a roof over my head. This entire time I searched Scripture, begging God to show me how I'm to be and what I'm supposed to do. Prayer was one, interceding for people. So, I prayed and prayed and prayed. First Peter was another answer to my prayer for direction, my attitude, and my heart. The Lord showed me how I am to be faithful as the only Christian among non-Christians. There was a girl who lived with us that didn't believe in Christ who I will call Sandy, plus Annabeth, David, and Alex. Four people who I prayed for regularly. They actively did not love Jesus. Later I found out that Annabeth practiced Wicca in her house and had actually read tarot cards to my son. She believed in tarot cards to predict the future and so many other things that were far from Christ.

There was a spiritual battle going on among us. I didn't see it but I knew it was there. Such darkness David let in, and the girls too. I prayed and prayed for Jesus to save them, to transform their hearts. I still pray for them.

I clung to Jesus most of the time, but at other moments, my desperation grew into depression.

Posted on Facebook/Instagram

April 4, 2020

Depression, anxiety, and suicide are real things. I've known five people who have killed themselves in the past five years. If you've ever even thought about taking your own life, please don't allow your thoughts to become reality. Let someone tell you about Jesus and the hope, refuge, strength, and love we find in Him. I know what it's like to be alone in my room for the past two years.

I've been at home, alone, for the past two years. My husband works and my son goes to school. I've been alone in my room. I know what you're feeling. I know what it's like not to go to church. For some of you this season is super busy, with kids at home and work at home too. But for some of you this is a lonely season. I feel your pain.

The Lord has gifted me with a heart to pray. So, I'm praying for you if you're lonely, depressed, sad, anxious, suicidal, or broken. I will point you to Jesus for His Spirit resides inside me and I'm never alone even when I feel lonely.

National Suicide Prevention Lifeline
Call 1 (800) 273-8255

Journal entries

April 5, 2020

My instructions from David and Annabeth regarding how I am to survive due to COVID:

Avoid everyone; they could be sick and not know
Especially Alex
I can schedule video calls with Alex
Text Alex anytime

Eat food and snacks inside my room
Walk ok
Stay in room for most of the day
I cannot go to Annabeth's house

Avoid Sandy
Distance 6 feet
No sharing food or drinks
Only prepare food for yourself in the microwave
Have Alex prepare his own food
Try not to touch your face
Don't walk through David's room, go around.
Leave Alex in his room till 8 am when David wakes him up.
Be sensitive to David's feelings of fear.
Realize that Alex is scared too and that he will miss me if I'm gone and worry about making me die.

Annabeth who lived across the street texted this:

"And in response to your question about hugging Alex: Given that contact is the main way that Covid-19 spreads, Alex can either be able to safely touch you and only you, or he can safely touch all three of us. Going back and forth between us and you is unsafe since we need to be able to leave the house & that means we interact with other people. For your safety and for his mental health if you do get the virus, we need him to not be in the position of possibly carrying germs from us to you.

So, we made the hard call that Alex should be able to get human contact and safe people time from the three of us since we collectively have the energy and capacity to fulfill his people-based needs right now. This was not an easy decision to make. None of us like telling you that you can't touch him. But it's the only safe option for both you and him. I hope that clarifies why this is a long-term restriction."

These are the rules I have to abide by because I have to submit to David.

God's girl,
Molly

May 15, 2020

I was grumpy being stuck in my room today, or rather confined in my room. Above my table are a few verses that the Lord continues to use in my life. "Rejoice always." *Always, Lord? Even in COVID-19? Even without Alex hugging me and without intimacy with my husband? Even in the distance of my church and the people You love? Even with me not cooking? Even with me not cleaning? Even with me not serving? Even in the waiting? Even in my loneliness? Even in the stillness? Even in my quiet room? Even in everything that has gone on in my life? Yes, Lord. Always. You say Always and You mean Always. Help me rejoice in You ALWAYS.*

"Pray without ceasing." *Lord, really? I already prayed today. And yesterday. And the day before that. You want me to keep praying? But Lord I don't want to. I want to be helping people, showing them You, writing Instagram messages, showing them pictures of Your beauty, or doing SOMETHING other than praying.*

I pray and pray and pray. And You don't seem to do anything about it. You still do whatever You want. Bad things in my life happen. Horrible things happen in other people's lives too. Particularly for Your people around the globe living in persecuted nations. And You're calling me to pray? It seems so unimportant. I should be going out there and doing something, anything. But no. I'm quarantined in my house. Away from everyone. And You tell me to pray. Without ceasing.

Lord, help me want to pray. Help me desire to pray. Help me to be overcome by praying. Help me to admit that doing "something," doing "anything" is not what You want for me. You've called me to let go of so many things and I have let go of them, or at least I stopped doing them in obedience to my husband. You've called me to surrender to You. I think I have.

And You've called me to pray. So Lord, yes, Father. I will pray and ask You to do a lot. Ask You to create in me a clean heart, Oh Lord. Ask You to stir up in me a passion for Your name. Ask You to move in a mighty way. Ask You to transform Your people. Ask You to save my friends and family. Ask You to do miracles in dark, ugly places. Ask You to sanctify Your people. Ask You to make us more in Your image. Ask You to work. Ask You to do SOMETHING, ANYTHING, for Your name Jesus, Your glory, Father God, and Your way, Holy Spirit. In Jesus' name, amen.

"Give thanks in all circumstances for this is the will of God in Christ Jesus for you" (1 Thessalonians 5:16-18). The Lord convicted me about this and I made this list for COVID-19:

1. Walk/talk/move hand
2. Alex is home
3. Married to David
4. David takes care of me
5. David and friends bringing me food
6. David stays up at night to make sure I'm ok
7. Communicate through writing
8. Sandy and Annabeth for taking care of me
9. Caitlin for cleaning our house
10. Alex for playing games & watching TV in the morning
11. That I'm not sick in the hospital
12. Friends
13. Family
14. Liz, that we get to pray
15. The cool temperature
16. Sunrises and sunsets
17. The beautiful and safe walks in the morning
18. The birds chirp and kitties roam the area
19. I can paint
20. I can watch TV and play games on my phone
21. Sandy & Annabeth cooking for our family
22. Granola bars that I have in the morning
23. Nurses and doctors helping people
24. Ambulance and paramedics
25. People that clean the hospital
26. Hospital workers
27. Grocery & fast-food workers

28. Friends for taking care of my son
29. Delivery drivers
30. People getting food for people
31. Pharmacy & workers for making sure medicine is right
32. Cookies
33. City group ladies for their honesty and walking with me through life
34. Prayer
35. People who pray for me
36. Pastor Jim for following God's lead
37. The word of God for being alive & not dead
38. Memorizing Scripture with the Ladies
39. My discipleship group
40. Books I've read of people's faith in Jesus
41. The persecuted church that clings to Jesus
42. Roses that my neighbors have and my parents send me pictures of
43. Technology
44. Duo & Zoom calls

June 25, 2020

Dear Lord, why is COVID-19 still going on? Why have You not shown people the cure? Why are so many people dying? Why are David and his girlfriends so afraid Alex will pass it on to me and cause my death?

How long must I be in my room and not touch anyone? Why is the lack of physical touch so depressing to me? Is it because Christian prisoners have no physical touch a lot of times?

Why am I alive and here on this Earth? Is it to write? Is it to be in Your presence? Please answer me. I beg You to listen. Understand. Empathize. Rescue me from myself and help me to be obedient. Please help me to know You and to crave to know you more.

Please help me to be submissive to my husband. Please help Alex to hug them a lot since he can't hug me. Please wrap Your arms around me as I cry tears of sorrow. Please show me You are right by my side always. Please be faithful. Please. In Jesus' name amen.

Thank You for this quote from "Heaven" by Randy Alcorn:

> I know that depression can be debilitating. Many godly people have experienced it. But if you are considering taking your own life, recognize this as the devil's temptation. Jesus said that Satan is a liar and murderer (John 8:44). He tells lies because he wants to destroy you (1 Peter 5:8). Don't listen to the liar. Listen to Jesus, the Truth Teller (John 8:32; 14:6).

God's girl,
Molly

❧ ☙

Chapter 16

Freedom

How much mercy and grace is too much? God has gifted me with a huge heart for the broken. I've shown mercy to David again, again, and again. So many times I've forgiven his mistakes. With God, I wrestled with figuring out when to stop showing David mercy. When can I get out? Should I even imagine life outside these walls?

August 23, 2020

Here I am, Lord, broken and in need of YOUR help. Please speak and help me to listen. Please guide me about separating with David.

Lord, Jane my sister has been asking me to divorce David, and many people in my city group have suggested I move out. Is it wise to separate? What about Alex? In Jesus' name, amen.

God's girl,
Molly

August 25, 2020

Here I am, LORD. You know exactly what today was all about. You knew that this day would happen before I was born. Thank You. Thank You for loving me when David doesn't love me anymore. Thank You for rescuing me even when the one I need rescuing from is David. Thank You that I finally said it out loud that David has abused me verbally, mentally, emotionally, and spiritually.

He screams and cusses at me, saying F*ck you and F*ck Jesus. He manipulates everything. He lies. And he lies. And he lies some more. I know he lies because I locked my door and asked him if I slept well last night, and he replied that I actively woke him up and went outside and acted crazy—when I KNOW I was locked inside my room all night.

Three doctors: my general practitioner, my neurologist, and my neuropsychologist, all say I do not have Alzheimer's. But David is convinced I have it because a nurse said I might have Alzheimer's. Doctors and scans say I'm fine—just forgetful. *What do I do, Lord?*

God's girl,
Molly

August 26, 2020

Here I am, broken and grieving. Please speak.

I read John 15 and Psalm 89.

Please, Lord, may this Psalm in the Passion be evident of me today—verse 8 and 17 in particular:

> So awesome are you, O Yahweh, Lord God of Angel Armies! Where could we find anyone as glorious as you? Your faithfulness shines all around you! …The glory of your splendor is our strength, and your marvelous favor makes us even stronger, lifting us even higher!

Please show Your favor to me, for possibly moving me out.

Thank You for Psalm 89:24, 33. "Because I [God] love him and treasure him, My faithfulness will always protect him. I will place My great favor upon him, and I will cause his power and fame to increase…. But I will never, no never, lift my faithful love from off their lives. My kindness will prevail and I will never disown them."

Thank You that Your faithful love will never leave. Thank You that You never lie but always speak the truth.

Thank You for the Passion's John 15:26, 27: "And I will send you the Divine Encourager from the very presence of my Father. He will come to you, the Spirit of Truth, emanating from the Father, and he will speak to you about me. And you will tell everyone the truth about me, for you have walked with me from the start."

I'm crying now tears of joy, thank You.

God's girl,
Molly

August 27, 2020

Here I am, meditating on TPT's Psalm 90. Please speak.

Oh thank You, Jesus, from the first verse You spoke – Psalm 90:1 "Lord, you have always been our eternal home, our hiding place from generation to generation." *Thank You that heaven is my eternal home. Thank You that I get to be forever with You by my side. You have carried me throughout my life and You are holding me still. You are my hiding place—now more than ever. Please hold me tight. I can't see You but I know You are there. Jehovah Shammah, the LORD is there. I do believe; help my unbelief. I surrender to You once again. Psalm 90:14 is my cry today.*

> Let the sunrise of your love end our dark night. Break through our clouded dawn again! Only you can satisfy our hearts, filling us with songs of joy to the end of our days.

Yes, Lord! Verse 15 reads, "We've been overwhelmed with grief…"

Yes, Lord! "...come now and overwhelm us with gladness..."

Oh, Father God, I don't know if I'm ready to say that yet. "... Replace our years of trouble with decades of delight."

Oh Spirit, I wept when I read that line. Please, Lord!

God's girl,

Molly

Later that day

I approached David and asked him if he would like a new wedding ring since his is broken. He said no and he didn't want to be married to me anymore, that he was done with me and that he preferred to be with his girlfriends rather than me. I knew that the three of them were sleeping together but I couldn't prove it. He said that everything that had happened turned out hard on him. He played the victim and said that he wanted to do things his way.

I said, "Thank you for being honest with me," and I closed my door. All of a sudden, freedom entered my body and I sighed out of relief. I cried uncontrollably and decided that I was going to leave

David's house that week. David, Annabeth and Sandy were staying at a vacation house, so it was just Alex and me home all week. Sandy stayed here the first few nights and then David stayed the last night.

I was so scared of him that I quietly packed and prayed the whole time. I fasted. I called my parents, pastor, discipleship group, sister, and told them the truth while hiding in the closet, away from David.

I called my aunt who is a divorce lawyer and she gave me advice that I quickly followed. She said I needed to get out of there within two days and I had already been packing. She said to delete my Facebook and Instagram accounts as soon as possible. The timing was completely God ordained because they were gone from my house and I could sneak and pack everything I desperately needed. I didn't sleep Thursday night, but fasted and packed.

Alex was the reason I had stayed married the past four years. That week I prayed for the Lord to show me whether or not Alex was coming with me to my cousin Iris' home. As I prayed, that week David and Sandy did not do anything with Alex. They just left him to fend and feed himself, checking on Alex a few times that week. David had stayed across the street at Annabeth's house. I then took care of Alex, even though I wasn't allowed to touch him or go within 6 feet of him. He was only nine years old. I decided he was coming with me and I would fight to keep him.

Thursday night, August 27, 2020, David showed up for a brief period and noticed my light was on at 10 pm. He knocked on my door and I panicked. I peeked out the door, with my back hiding my packing. David asked me if I was ok and I explained that I couldn't sleep, which was honestly true. He said he hoped I slept.

He took Alex out at that point, and panic again overtook me thinking that I would never see Alex again. The Lord reassured me that I had to let go and surrender everything over to Him. Surrender meant having faith in Jesus. Surrender meant trusting Jesus.

So I did. Iris, my cousin, was coming in the morning and I would hopefully leave with Alex, but I didn't know if it was going to happen. Fear drove me and I had to give that fear over to Jesus to help me once again. I surrendered time and time again. Trusting Jesus.

Six am Friday came and I walked into Alex's room. He was sleeping and I thanked Jesus for placing him in my house and not in Annabeth's.

August 28, 2020

At 6:30 am I quietly woke up Alex and said, "We're going to Iris' house for the week. I need you to pack your clothes, your stuffed animals, your favorite toys, and your school books. Put them in your backpacks and when you run out of room, I have trash bags you could use. I know you have a lot of questions, and I will answer them when we get into Iris' car."

Alex asked if Dad knows. I replied, "No, he does not know and that's why I need you to be extra quiet so we don't wake up Dad who is sleeping in Sandy's room."

He asked some more questions, to which I replied "Do you trust me?" Alex said yes. I said, "Good. Then please listen to what I say and remember to be as quiet as possible. I love you so much. And we can touch now."

Alex looked puzzled and said, "Does Dad say we can touch?" "No," I replied, "but I say we can." He jumped out of bed and said, "It's about time." We embraced for the first time since March—five months ago, five long and heart-wrenching months. We quietly packed everything we needed and fled David's house.

I left David a note that said we're leaving for my cousin Iris' house for the week to think about what he said. And Alex is staying with us for at least a week. I took a picture of the note

Iris and her husband Larry came and loaded everything in their cars. A friend came by and brought me the essential items I needed. As soon as we got into Larry's car, I explained to Alex that his Daddy and I were getting divorced. I expressed that I loved his dad so much. We both loved Alex but Jesus loved him even more. I knew he had a lot of questions and fears, it's ok, I had fears too. I was never going back to that house. It was not Alex's fault at all, just his daddy and I had separated. It was nothing Alex did or could do. I was moving in with Iris and not coming back to that house again. Alex was coming with me for a week or two. I was not taking Alex away from his dad. We'd figure out a way that he could stay with his dad for a while and me for a while.

Iris and I had decided that we would spend the first night at the home of her friend who was unknown to David. My Uncle Silas stood guard back at Iris' house that day. We dropped off Alex at her friend's house so we could focus on the immediate priorities.

Looking back, I was stunned to finally see God's master plan in action for just this moment. I had so many knowledgeable contacts through the New Life Ministry who guided me through my own successful escape plan. One lady highly recommended a lawyer for us to use. Since the COVID restrictions were still in full force, I met remotely with the lawyer she recommended. He was available that morning and walked me through the action steps I needed to take that day. My parents and I arranged for a wire transfer that paid his retainer.

With fear and trembling, Iris and I went to the bank where I had access to the one account into which David deposited the grocery money each month. I pulled out $270 and left $1 in my account.

Around 10 am I was talking to my lawyer when I had an incoming call from David. My lawyer advised me not to answer his call and not to even read the messages. He explained that I'm an adult who told David I was going to my cousin's house with Alex for the week.

David called me about 15 times, texted me, left three messages, called Iris, and texted her. He was very explicit and demanded that I return our son. He cussed me out and said a lot of other things I cannot write here.

This was the scariest part of that day, especially since David regularly used my phone to track my location and often hacked into my text messages. He's brilliant and relentless that way. I of course denied him access, but we decided the safest place to stop might be the parking lot at the local police station. When we settled there, I called my lawyer again and discussed strategy with him.

I was terrified that David would become violent, so my lawyer arranged for me to get a restraining order while we sat at the police station and I received it electronically.

On my aunt's advice, I also deleted my Facebook and Instagram accounts.

My dad and my aunt arranged for me to get a new phone and a computer, to replace the phone David knew about. Later at Iris' house, I saved all the text messages that David had sent me to give my lawyer proof that David abused me mentally, verbally, and psychologically. Then I only used that phone to contact David.

As my remote meeting with my lawyer ended, my lawyer said I could text David back ….so I did:

"David, please stop texting and calling me. I am fine. Alex is with me and he's fine. He's having fun. He will be at my cousin's house with me. Do not come here—I don't want to see you. I will communicate with you next week. Please stop calling me. Respect my request to be left alone."

He replied immediately and cursed at me again. When he showed up at Iris' house, Uncle Silas firmly told him to leave. The house would be protected, and Alex and I would be defended if he returned. David left.

Once again, the Lord asked me to let go and surrender everything over to Him. I let go of David and his numerous messages, surrendering him to Jesus. Later I found out that the lawyer we had hired was one of David's friends. That night, David called him to be his lawyer but he couldn't because I was his client. My lawyer was shocked by my story. He had no idea of the abuse that David had inflicted on me. He also didn't know that David had slept with two of his gal friends, who I called his girlfriends.

Due to my now lack of Facebook/Instagram friends, I set up an email group for people who prayed for me after I separated from David. I'm so thankful for the people of God who supported me, comforted me, and helped me process the recovery.

Most importantly, they prayed. Talking to God is so vital and it was the only thing that got me through this hard season. I prayed a lot, but there's something in the joining together with other people in prayer that was necessary for at least my recovery.

I needed God, desperately. Clinging to Him got me through. I knew I needed His help and I asked people to pray especially for me about 1-3 times a week. They encouraged me greatly. They also provided for me and financially helped me when I had no money of my own. A lot of friends pitched in to buy me a car too, for which I'm so grateful!

I was able to sleep after I left David, like up to eleven hours a night! I found out that Annabeth kept me on a small dosage of my sleeping meds and after I corrected it, I slept fine. It was nice to disconnect from social media for a time. Alex and I spent quality time together without me looking down at my phone. I no longer felt pressured to be a certain way.

I went to counseling and got to talk about David with her. She helped me process everything. I remember walking into church on Sunday for the first time in two years. I was overjoyed to be with my fellow believers worshiping God with them. I really felt encouraged and my passion for Jesus ignited (Hebrews 10:23, 24). I joined the prayer team at my church and began interceding with people.

Below are a few emails I sent to my prayer partners

September 2, 2020

Hi everyone,

This is my prayer warriors' team. Thank you so much for being a part of this ministry!

I do not have Alzheimer's according to my doctor, my neurologist and my neuropsychologist. David just said I did; he lied about that and made me feel guilty about it. As of Friday morning, I left David's house and am seeking a divorce. I packed up my belongings (journals/clothes/paintings) and quietly took them to my cousin Iris's house. I took Alex with me and had him pack his favorite toys, clothes, and school books.

Today I'm taking Alex to the doctor's office and having our doctor explain why I don't have Alzheimer's, am not high risk for COVID-19, and I'm capable of taking care of Alex. Please pray:

Prayer requests

Alex: He would believe the truth
He would have peace
He would understand what the doctor says

Me: Wisdom to help Alex and not burden him
God would give me grace for David
That I would have the Lord's strength

God's girl,
Molly

September 3, 2020

Thank you all for praying for me! Alex and I went to see my nurse practitioner, Jack, who has known us for six years. David trusts him. I trust him. I wrote down questions and I asked Jack:

1. My husband has told Alex that I have Alzheimer's. Is that correct?

– He answered no. "She had a stroke and this medicine she's taking helps her brain work faster. She is fully capable of taking care of herself and him. Her neurologist who specializes in brain activities has scanned her and she does not have Alzheimer's disease."

2. My husband told Alex that I could die sooner because of my Alzheimer's. Am I in danger of dying?

– He answered no. "She could die in a car crash, but everyone could die in a car crash. Your mom is not going to die anytime soon because if she was, I would see her more often."

3. During COVID-19 from March until now, I (Molly) had to stay in my room and could only come out one time a day. Since then, I have not touched or come within 6 feet of Alex or anyone else. Is that necessary and does Alex need to worry about getting me sick?

– He answered No. I'm more likely to get COVID-19 because I see people who are positive COVID-19. And I have two girls who want to hug me as soon as I get home from work, but I don't hug them until I change my clothes, take a shower, and make sure I don't have any germs on me. And then we hug.

I cannot even imagine what it was like not to have your mom hug you. Your mom is smart, she's wearing a good mask, you're wearing a good mask, she doesn't come in contact with anyone who has COVID-19, you haven't come into contact with anyone who has COVID-19, and there is no way that you could cause her to get it."

4. My husband told Alex that he could cause me to die if he got close. Can you help him with that?

– Jack did help me with this and he talked about how Alex being close to me will not cause me to die.

5. If Alex has any more questions can he ask you? Like in the future?

"Absolutely. Your mom contacts me through this app and I answer her back within the same day. You can ask anything you want. Like are you scared right now?" Alex started crying.

"Yes," Alex said.

"That's ok. It's perfectly normal for you to be scared. What are you afraid about?" Jack said.

"I could lose everything that I own because dad would get rid of it," Alex said.

We both assured him that it's ok to be scared. Mom is scared too. We will try to get him everything back and Daddy will let you spend the night with him. The lawyer is going to help us figure all that stuff out.

6. I also asked him if I could go to Target to get some things we need and he said absolutely.

That was it. Afterwards, Iris drove us to Target. I pray that Alex would not feel like he has to please me or David, which I've told him all week. We're not in control, God is in control. He sees the past, present, and future. He knows the truth and what is happening. And I trust Him.

God's girl,
Molly

September 10, 2020

Hi everyone,

I'm very weak right now and tempted to give in to fear. I talked with my lawyer and David hired a female lawyer to divorce me and claims I'm not able to care for my child. He claimed I'm incompetent—not able to cook, drive, walk, talk, and that I have Alzheimer's.

He claims to be able to take care of Alex even though the last week I lived in that house he only was home for about an hour that week and took Alex skateboarding for an hour. Sandy slept in till 1 pm every day. David slept with Annabeth in the mountains the first night, stayed at her house during the day/night, and only came home to sleep in Sandy's room Thursday night—the last night while I packed everything and took Alex to Iris' house.

From 6 am-1 pm every day I made sure Alex did his school. I talked, played with, and took care of my son even though I wasn't able to touch him because of David's rules. He fed Alex at 9 pm or 10 pm every night and didn't bother about lunch or breakfast. I'm the one who made sure Alex ate.

Pray that I would place my faith in Jesus.

Pray I will trust Jesus.

Pray that I will believe the truth over lies.

Pray that my lawyer would recognize the truth and recognize lies.

Pray that the judge would recognize truth over lies.

Pray that the truth will set me free and that justice will be served.

Pray that Alex recognizes truth over lies.

Pray that I will receive justice over the oppression that David has had me under.

Pray that Alex will ultimately realize that God is in control and not David.

Pray for peace in my heart and Alex's heart.

Thank you so much!
God's girl,
Molly

September 14, 2020

Hello everyone.

Thank you all for your prayers and financial help! I'm in awe that God has all the money in the world and that He would provide for me abundantly. He has protected me and Alex. He is glorious, good, faithful, just, and loving.

I have good moments, sad moments, overwhelmed moments, angry moments, joyful moments, and just about every moment you could think of. I'm doing much better since I last emailed. The Lord humbled me and made me realize that I cannot do this on my own but need His help. He is so strong and is able to defend me against David and his oppression. The Lord has taught me about surrendering to Him again and again in suffering.

Praise—We figured out a school schedule where I'm teaching Alex and correcting his workbooks.

Praise—Alex and I will share a room with a bunk bed, couch, my TV, a new closet system, book shelf, and dresser. I purchased all of that through the money that you all sent. Thank you! We finished painting our room green, and we're both happy with the decision we made.

Praise—I have my aunt's Mac laptop and it's mine. For ten years I have not had a Mac even though David purchased a Mac laptop for three people he knows and himself four times.

Prayer—Lawyer and I are meeting for the first time to go over expenses, what I need from David's house, figuring out Alex and who he's staying with, and we're setting up an "inventory and appraisement." Pray for that?

Pray I get everything done with the lawyer, Alex's school, and I also rest and refocus on Jesus. The Spirit has shown me throughout this messy divorce process that God ultimately will be glorified. Justice will be served, if not here on earth, then in Heaven.

God's girl,
Molly

September 17, 2020

Hello everyone,

Praise—We finished another week of school! I spent 3-4 hours a day teaching the three boys, plus lawyer calls/emails/forms, plus cooking, plus a ton of extra stuff. The Lord continues to give me the grace and strength to accomplish all of that. Praise Jesus!

Praise—I still have slept EVERY night 7-11 hours. Praise Jesus!

Prayer—Alex is spending time with David tomorrow & Sunday from 10 am - 8 pm. I'm nervous, overwhelmed, and anxious about seeing David for the first time tomorrow. Our lawyers had us sign documents stating that David would Facetime Alex alone from 6 pm - 6:30 pm on weekdays. And David gets to see Alex. Pray that his time with his dad is fun and not burdensome.

Prayer—Family court services ordered Alex to see a counselor early next week. Wisdom in the courts deciding who/what/when/where. Grace and freedom for Alex to talk openly. Peace for me.

Thank you for all your prayers! I would not survive if Jesus wasn't good and faithful. But He is and I'm so thankful!

God's girl,

Molly

September 20, 2020

Hi everyone,

Thank you for praying!! The Lord carried us through yesterday. Alex had a great time with his dad. I saw him, with my mask on, and him three cars away from me (I have a restraining order against him). My Uncle Silas drove us there and stood facing David. I'm so grateful for his support.

David talked briefly about Alex having no shoes to skateboard with and how he needed to get some. Then Alex left without giving me a hug. I immediately raced to the car, and pounded on the door. Then David responded to my knock on the door asking for Alex to give me a hug with, "Well that's rude, you forgot to hug your mom!" At which, I embraced my son and thought with anger to myself, "You didn't let Alex TOUCH ME FOR MONTHS!!" …. but the Lord helped me keep my mouth shut.

Uncle Silas and I picked up Alex at 8 pm. He had fun with his dad, and only his dad because the other girls weren't there. Praise—I'm so thankful that the two girls listened to my lawyer and did not come near my son. Praise Jesus!

Then Uncle Silas and I took Alex at 10 am this morning and we're picking him up at 8 pm.

The Lord is my strength and fear has disappeared for the moment. I know and see Him protecting me, guiding me, directing me, and loving me.

- Pray that Alex sees that side of God too.
- Pray that the Lord would help Alex depend on Him.
- Pray that David repents and turns to Jesus.
- Pray that the two girls would repent and turn away from their sins.
- Pray that the Lord would continue to be my everything.

Thank you for your prayers!
God's girl,
Molly

September 27, 2020

Hello everyone,

Thanks for praying for me! This morning I read Psalm 121 in the Passion Translation. I highlighted every verse and am so thankful that our Lord is my Protector, keeper, "Guardian God" who will never forget me or ignore me.

Praise—Still sleeping about 8 hours a night. Praise Jesus! I've never done that before.

Prayer—Car that I CAN DRIVE. Pray for the finances that I have, pray for me to somehow get a car, pray for the safety of driving for me, pray that I would focus on my surroundings while driving. I've never had my own car before, always shared one with David. Two years ago, David bought a car with a stick shift, which I can't drive because of my stroke.

Prayer—On Monday we're calling to see if I can get on disability. David said that I didn't qualify because I only worked for my dad. But I've never called them so I pray and ask you to pray that I can get it.

Prayer—Family Court services are having Alex interviewed next week to determine what happened between David and me as well as schooling for Alex. Pray that I would still be able to homeschool our son. Pray for the truth to be revealed. Pray that Alex doesn't feel like he has to choose sides.

Prayer—Strength, endurance, perseverance, comfort, energy, faith in Jesus, that I would no longer believe the lies that David told me about myself and everything else.

Thank You!

God's girl,

Molly

September 30, 2020

Hello all,

At the moment, I need the Lord's help, energy, clarity, wisdom, direction, and mercy. Pray for that for me?

Prayer—that I would have enough money. I must confess I'm anxious about that. I thought I would start getting child support from David at the end of the month because we had the court date. But it's been postponed. Pray that I will trust Christ and remember that HE has all the money in the world and will provide for us. And pray for Him to provide.

Prayer—Alex realized that I'm not going back to David's house and he's sad about that. Pray for grace and mercy for Alex.

Prayer—Still homeschooling Alex and, man, do I respect my own mom so much! She put up with my sister and me, homeschooling us for years. Pray that I will have the patience, motivation, and wisdom to teach my son? Pray that he would do his school work, not grumble about it, and be eager to learn.

Thank you all so much!

God's girl,

Molly

October 2, 2020

Hello everyone,

How are you all doing? My life was a mess all week and yet I'm deeply encouraged by all of you. This morning I read Proverbs 12 to my son. We stopped reading to discuss many of the verses and Proverbs 12:25 reminded me of you all. The Passion Translation puts it, "Anxious fear brings depression [which I struggled with when living with David], but a life-giving word of encouragement can do wonders to restore joy to the heart."

Thank you for giving me encouraging words, words of affirmation and not condemnation, reminding me of the TRUTH and not telling me lies, being gentle with me and not always over correcting me by bringing me down with your tone of voice like David did. Thank you, my fellow body of believers, for surrounding me with love, joy, tears, financial help, and encouragement.

God's girl,
Molly

❧ ☙

At this point I became overwhelmed emotionally. My friend Amy sat me down and encouraged me to talk with a counselor. I searched and researched counselors. After much prayer, I talked with a Christian woman I shall call Rebecca. Over the course of a year, she helped me discern between truth and lies. Lies that David told me and I believed, such as, I was incapable of teaching my son, I was not able to drive, and I was unable to be around lots of people, or so I thought. Rebecca, along with my doctors, helped me see that I could teach my son. That I could drive. That I could be with my church family.

November 8, 2020

Dear prayer people,

I am overwhelmed by weariness and mental, emotional, spiritual, and psychological exhaustion. I sleep fine (praise Jesus!), but I'm tempted to be overcome by my life. My city group brought me a few meals and that really helped. But I still need Jesus and to be satisfied with His love.

I crave intimacy, I long to be fulfilled. I'm tempted to go out and meet a true Christian man who works hard and will provide for us. I long to be kissed and held and even touched by a man. David hadn't done that for years. I crave physical contact. I'm tempted. But God has already shown me that HE IS MORE THAN ENOUGH.

I read Psalm 63 this morning, starting at verse 1. I long for God, but He feels distant. My soul thirsts for Jesus, but my mouth is dry. "O God, you are my God; earnestly I seek you; my soul thirsts for you; my flesh faints for you, as in a dry and weary land where there is no water."

- Pray—I will follow Him despite my weariness.
- Pray—Jesus holds me tight.
- Pray—I will not give in to temptation and have a suitor but be satisfied with Jesus' love.
- Pray—The Lord will heal me mentally, emotionally, spiritually, and psychologically.
- Praise—I got my first child support check! The money will be tight but I'm thankful that David is paying me to take care of our son.
- Pray—Alex sees a counselor tomorrow morning at 9 am. Pray that he would tell her the truth. Pray that he opens up and shares his struggles. Pray that the Lord will use this for the good of Alex and not allow Satan a chance to win.
- Pray—The rest of Psalm 63:2-8 for me:

> So I have looked upon You in the sanctuary, beholding Your power and glory. Because Your steadfast love is better than life, my lips will praise You. So I will bless You as long as I live; in Your name I will lift up my hands. My soul will be satisfied as with fat and rich food, and my mouth will praise You with joyful lips, when I remember You upon my bed, and meditate on You in the watches of the night; for You have been my help, and in the shadow of Your wings I will sing for joy. My soul clings to You; Your right hand upholds me.

Thank you!
God's girl,
Molly

November 21, 2020

Dear Prayer people,

The Lord has blessed me with an abundance of His grace and mercy—by loving me when I sinned against Him, by embracing me with His compassion and gentleness, by providing more than enough for me to buy a car, by providing me with Iris' family and their welcoming home, and in so many other ways.

God is the richest in the world and I'm so thankful that He gave me enough money to buy a car THROUGH YOU ALL. Thank you for the money! I really appreciate it! I'll probably pick up the car later today and then I'll send you all a photo.

Praise—Sandy left David.

God's girl,

Molly

Chapter 17

Acceptance

Acceptance is hard. I wanted things to go my way, and they didn't exactly happen the way I thought was best. The Lord knows best and, as difficult as that is to admit, I began to trust Him more. I fought hard for the court to see that I could handle taking care of a child, my child. The Lord remained good no matter what happened. I can see now that His plan far exceeds my own ideas. Yet, in this time of my life I had to accept what Jesus wanted me to accept.

December 1, 2020

Hey everyone, I have an URGENT PRAYER REQUEST.

My preliminary court date is tomorrow and David has declared that he wants more custody of Alex and that he wants Alex to re-enter public school in Dallas. He is seeking to resist my primary custody and homeschooling of Alex. This is a bit unexpected for me, because I had thought that David was satisfied with weekend visits. If the court rules in his favor tomorrow, Alex will alternate spending whole weeks between my house and David's.

PLEASE PRAY…Please pray that the judge (whom my lawyer says may not be favorable in siding with me since I am disabled) would listen to my case and that I would find favor with her.

Pray that I would speak well and articulate for myself tomorrow.
Pray that the judge would see all of the abuse that David has done.
Pray that justice would be served.
Pray for Alex as he's the person that both of us are fighting over.
Pray for Alex to understand that the Lord is good and merciful.

Pray that I would not be afraid of the outcome and would trust God's goodness.

Pray that David would be humbled as he opposes me, makes our lives difficult, and runs from the Lord.

Pray that David repents of his sin, and emotional abuse of me.

Pray that the judge will see/act in Alex's best interest.

Pray that the Lord moves in a mighty way and contradicts Annabeth's tarot card reading of the situation.

Pray that the Lord is victorious and Satan loses mightily in this battle.

Pray that I would be reminded that this is a spiritual battle and pray that I will have enough faith to let go and trust Jesus.

Pray that I am reminded that Jesus wins in the end, no matter what.

Pray for a good night's sleep for both me and Alex.

Thank you so much prayer warriors. My court appointment is tomorrow at 10 am.

God's girl,
Molly

December 2, 2020 7:12am

Dear prayer warriors,

Thank you for praying! I prayed that the Lord would wake me up at 5 am so I could be alone with Him. He woke me up earlier, at 4:30/45 am, and I've been in my Bible and deep in prayer.

> If you bow low in God's awesome presence, he will eventually exalt you as you leave the timing in his hands. Pour out all your worries and stress upon him and leave them there, for he always tenderly cares for you. Be well balanced and always alert, because your enemy, the devil, roams around incessantly, like a roaring lion looking for its prey to devour. Take a decisive stand against him and resist his every attack with strong, vigorous faith. For you know that your believing brothers and sisters around the world are experiencing the same kinds of troubles you endure. And then, after your brief suffering, the God of all loving grace, who has called you to share in His eternal

> glory in Christ, will personally and powerfully restore you and make you stronger than ever. Yes, He will set you firmly in place and build you up. And He has all the power needed to do this—forever! Amen.
>
> *1 Peter 5:6-11 TPT*

I prayed this passage for me in my situation as well as for the countless other women (and men) who are also in similar situations across the globe. I know of women who are persecuted by their husbands and forced into unbearable living circumstances. I know of women whose husbands beat them because they wear a cross necklace or say the name of Jesus. I know of women who, unlike me, don't have as much support as I do from the body of believers.

I urge you to pray for me, yes, but also for them. For the broken, misunderstood, poor, persecuted who love Jesus and have everything taken away, including their livelihood/property/food—everything besides Jesus taken away. Pray for the people who are persecuted. Pray for justice and mercy for their persecutors. Pray for God to be by their side and fight for them. Pray for God to deliver them from Satan's grasp.

God's girl,
Molly

December 2, 2020 1:38 pm

Dear prayer warriors,

Thank you for praying! Well, the Lord answered our prayers in that I get Alex for most of the time. We argued back and forth between our lawyers. Unfortunately, Alex will spend from the 18th-25th of December at David's house. I'm working on it with my lawyer to figure out when Alex can see my Nani/Aunt/parents.

Prayers for that? I know it's utterly confusing, but thank you for praying because I got what I wanted. We met with the judge over Zoom and then another judge joined us over Zoom again and had the preliminary court date hearing today. Unfortunately, she's not available again until August 2021. So, we have until August (1 year since I left David) for our lawyers to decide (out of court). David also gave my lawyer all of his credit card usage and debts.

Basically, he's paying me child support and that is it until the lawyers decide what else he owes me.

Praise—God answered our prayers for Alex staying with me majority of the time, plus two weekends a month.

Praise—God still worked it out so that I can have some income through child support.

Praise—All his debt/what he owes the bank is under his coverage and not my responsibility.

Praise—I've lived off of nothing with David so I actually have a budget that I've worked out and can manage with only child support.

Praise—I just got my COVID testing and I tested NEGATIVE for Covid-19!!

Prayer—Pray for me to wait for my car. A friend and I have arranged to practice driving in the parking lot since it's been over three years since I've driven anywhere. Pray that I drive smoothly, don't wreck, am at peace and not so tense, watch my surroundings, and the Lord protects me and everyone else.

Prayer—Pray that I will enjoy the time alone on the weekends, and with Alex from Monday through Thursday.

Prayer/praise—The Lord would continue to be good, faithful, loving, just, merciful and righteous forever.

Thank you so much for your prayers!

God's girl,

Molly

December 5, 2020

Dear prayer warriors,

Thank you so much for praying for me! Well, I drove for the first time in three years…and the Lord protected me, the car, and everyone else. PRAISE the Lord. I just stayed on the backroads and it felt so good to be able to drive.

Thank you for providing money for the car! Thank you all for praying for me to drive safely. Thank you all for praying for us at the court hearing. I was a little emotional and not trusting God the next day. With Iris' encouragement, I was reminded to let go of ALL my anxieties and lay them down at Jesus' feet. Even if it meant that I wasn't going to see Alex on my birthday or Christmas.

The Lord answered a lot of your prayers and He allowed David to agree with me and let Alex visit my Nani, Aunty, and parents on the 20th from noon till eight pm. Thank you all for praying!

I pray that you all will enjoy your Christmas, whether you're with family or friends or all alone. I pray that you would remember that Jesus is forever faithful and with you even when you can't see Him. He is the same yesterday, today, and forever (Hebrews 13:8).

God's girl,
Molly

December 8, 2020

Dear Lord, I'm a mess right now. I have so many negative thoughts and replaying memories of the girls and David on my mind. Alex and I are home alone for the first time in my new status of single mom. He's pushing my buttons so much and last night I was so weary that I let him have his own way.

Lord, I read this morning about widows and those below 60 years old how they need to get married. I long for a marriage to be under Your guidance and will. I long for a husband who truly knows You and loves You and desires for me to love You too. I long for a man to take up the burden of raising my son to be Your son.

I long for a marriage, yet I also grieve my marriage to David not working out. I could list all the ways that my marriage was not according to Your will. I could blame David for his adultery, the "me first" attitude, the lies, and so much more sin. I could take the shame of not being pretty enough for him, that I'm nothing in comparison to those women he chose.

I could take the blame for my marriage not working out, but that is not what You've called me to do. I am weak and we both messed up. David messed up and I messed up. Alex is unfortunately in the middle and we're fighting over custody.

Please Lord, fight this battle, and let me remember that You already won this battle of sin and darkness. You are victorious. You, Jesus, are that One who died for all of our messed-up ways. You were pierced, You were mocked, You were stabbed, You were beaten, You were crucified, You were laid in a tomb. You did all of that because You loved us. You loved me. Thank You. Help me remember and cling to that.

Hold on to me because I am weak and tired. I can't do this alone and thank You that I'm not alone. Thank You for Your Spirit living inside of me. Thank You for all the Christians around the globe who are going through a difficult season. Thank You for the persecuted believers that You've reminded me of to keep praying for them. Help all of us know You are with us always. May we cling to You knowing that You hold us too. In Jesus' name, amen.

God's girl,
Molly

December 13, 2020

Dear prayer partners.

Thank You so much for partnering with me in prayer! I feel so loved and cared for through all of you. This week has been difficult and joyous.

Praise—The Lord answered yes to a lot of your prayers and also no to some. I'm sad that Alex isn't going to be with me for my birthday and Christmas. I had to let go of that and grieve. BUT the Lord knew that Alex would be at his Dad's house and He comforted me about letting go of my plans and accepting His plans. I praise Him in the storms of life because He is good even when bad things happen.

Praise—I'm driving and I haven't crashed my car! Praise Jesus! He has helped me drive only when I'm fully awake and aware of the surroundings. I feel like my car is a gigantic gift from all of you who donated money or prayed for me to get a car. Thank you so much!!

Pray that I would not fear the unknown, lay my fears down at His feet, let go of all my anxieties.

Pray that I take up my cross daily—die to self, say No to self and Yes to God.

Pray that I will be obedient.

Pray that the Lord would guide me, direct my steps, and I would use my time wisely.

Pray that God would provide for my needs and I would be wise with money.

Thank you all!

God's girl,
Molly

December 18, 2020

Well, my first Christmas and birthday without Alex or David has started. I dropped off Alex last night. I'm tempted to pout and ascertain a "woe is me," but that would be disobedience to God. Instead, the Lord led me to being thankful and writing it all down:

1. Thankful that God is almighty, powerful, loving, gracious, merciful, compassionate, refuge, safe haven, justice, deliverer, hiding place, the Lord who sees, hears, watches, knows all things.
2. Thankful that Jesus is my Savior—He died brutally on the cross for me and three days later He rose. He's my Shepherd, shelter, my protector and my redeemer.
3. Thankful Jesus is sitting at the right hand of the Father interceding for me.
4. Thankful that the Holy Spirit resides in me. He is my helper, counselor and not only does He intercede for me but He groans for me.
5. The Lord has helped me sleep at night 6-12 hours every single night, sometimes only waking up two times, which is huge because at David's house I would sleep maybe 3-5 hours with waking up 6-8 times. So I'm thankful for sleep.
6. Thankful that the Lord gave me freedom as soon as David said he didn't want to be married to me.
7. Thankful that the Lord made it all work out with packing all my stuff and taking it out of the house while David was sleeping.
8. Thankful that Alex was awakened and we immediately hugged, for the first time since March (5 months).
9. Thankful that Alex helped me pack all my things and take them outside.
10. Thankful that Iris and Larry helped me move out.
11. Thankful for the joy of Alex in the midst of grieving the loss of my husband.
12. Thankful for all the love and support I received from family and friends.
13. Thankful for the money & gift cards I got to spend that family and friends gave me.

14. Thankful for all the gifts, furniture, and clothes I received from family and friends.
15. Thankful that Jesus was born in a dirty manger, not in a perfect castle.
16. Thankful for my car that was given to me from family and friends.
17. Thankful for my counselor and the safe place I can talk.
18. Thankful for all the emotional and spiritual support.
19. Thankful for my parents paying for my divorce.
20. Thankful for the great recommendation for a lawyer.
21. Thankful that my Nani, aunt, uncle, and parents are coming to visit.
22. Thankful that Alex gets to see them all tomorrow from noon—8pm.
23. Thankful that I get to spend Christmas with my parents and family and for all their support.
24. Thankful that my Christmas is not about buying the most expensive gifts.
25. Thankful that Jesus came to earth and was born as a baby.
26. Thankful that Jesus is my reason for the season.
27. Iris' kitchen where I get to make all sorts of yummy food.
28. Thankful that I get to bake and cook.
29. Thankful that Larry washes my dishes if I cook for the family.
30. Thankful that God is good and He gives me good gifts.

Merry Christmas!
God's girl,
Molly

December 22, 2020

Dear Jesus, I just went to the church planting meeting for Dallas. Do You want Alex and me to go? They're planting right in the poorer neighborhood, that spot Mom M and I used to go shopping. You have always called me in the past to poorer rather than richer. East of Dallas is richer. I wanted to live here but now I don't know. Please show me if You would have us in Dallas. Please guide and direct us and other people regarding this church plant. In Jesus' name, amen.

God's girl,
Molly

December 23, 2020

Today was a good but hard day. I'm 31 today. I didn't even see David today and I don't think I even want to see my husband, soon to be ex-husband. I got to see Alex for 30 minutes on Google Duo and I cried when he hung up.

Oh Lord, I'm right now holding back tears. I had a great morning celebrating my birthday with my parents but now it's hard with Alex away. Please comfort me, Jesus. I need You to hold me, Lord. Let me cry tears on Your shoulders, hearing the beating of Your heart, Jesus. I'm just sad today. Please shower me with Your tender love through Your Word. In Jesus' name, amen.

Thank You Jesus for speaking to me through Your Word. Thank You that in the Bible King David went through a hard time when the Philistines captured him in Gath and he wrote Psalm 56. Thank You for verse 8. You do count my every tear. Lord, thank You for recording them all in Your book.

Oh I'm so sad and I miss Alex! My baby. Yet, I know that it was Your will that we're apart now. You knew of this day before I carried Alex in my womb. You knew and You cared. You see me and listen because of Your love for me. I do have hope in You.

I don't see why this is happening but I do praise You even in this storm. I praise You for You are good. Yet even still You keep track of my tears because You care. I do praise You. I do trust in Your Word. Thank You, Holy Spirit, for Your prayers of compassion. In Your name, amen.

God's girl,
Molly

Psalm 91:1
Whoever dwells in the shelter of the Most High will rest in the shadow of the Almighty.

February 7, 2021

I feel like sh*t. I feel like cussing; I want to scream and yell and throw profanity at the wall. But I'm not. Let's back up and write through this crap. It all started with a movie of a physically and mentally abusive husband to his wife. It hit me hard and I cried because I flashed back to all the times David yelled and cussed at me. He said f*ck you and listed all the "selfish" things I've done to humiliate him. So many times I cried after he left. I wasn't about to cry in his presence after that traumatic time when he belittled me and called me weak.

I'm mad at David. I wish he could see how small he's made me feel. I wish he could understand the length my love for him went. I wish he even knew a little bit how difficult trying to find a job was going to be for me after I left. I wish he knew his own selfishness. I wish he knew I went above and beyond trying to please him.

I wish he knew the extent of how self-centered his money spending habits were. I wish he could see the pride he stuffed down my throat every time I even mentioned something. I wish he knew how little he made me feel and the gravity of the "All that *I've* done for you."

I wish he knew a fraction of the literal pain my stroke and heart surgery were. Fast forward ten years, I wish he knew how difficult it is for me to find a job with my disabled hand and difficulty speaking or remembering words.

I wish he knew how difficult it was for me to have a husband who touched me in front of people but when we're alone he slept on the couch and refused to even hug me. It's like he changed into a different man.

I wish he saw what I feel. All this anger. All this rage. I'm normally a "nice" person, but, man, am I on fire today.

I talked to an old friend whose husband is an alcoholic and abusive, more so than David. It blew my mind that she feels the same way that I do, or did—trapped and trying to protect my son. I talked to another lady whose husband mentally and psychologically abused her for twenty years. A dear friend was physically abused for thirty years and her husband had 100 sexual relationships with men and women. Another man I talked to was abused by his wife. And on and on it goes.

God comforts me as *El Roi* who sees me, knows me, hears me, watches me, embraces me, and loves me. He sees you, knows you, hears you, watches you, embraces you, and loves you. Over the years, I've personally talked to some women and men who were in abusive relationships. I've always cautioned people to get out of their marriages or relationships when I notice certain "red" flags. I've talked to adults, some in their 30's or 60's whose dads/moms or step-dads abused them. I've talked with some children who were abused and helped them get out. Or prayed that they would get out.

And here I am, having personally been abused, mistreated, and misunderstood. Only God knows the bruises I have emotionally. Only God knows all the bruises people have emotionally, physically, psychologically, and spiritually. Only He knows.

A friend of mine told me the Lord comforts her as *El Roi*, the God who sees.

In the Old Testament this name of God appears after a bit of a rivalry between Abraham's wife, Sarah, and Hagar. The whole story is a mess. Basically Abraham, at the time called Abram and his wife known as Sarai, had a great promise from God found in Genesis 12:3 that He would bless Abram and, "I will bless those who bless you and him who dishonors you I will curse…" In Genesis 15:5 and 6, He promised that Abram would have so many children, that they would become "a great nation whose descendants are as numerous as the stars."

Only the couple had tried and tried to conceive and failed. This was years before infertility treatment. No child came. He was 75 years old and his wife 66. And yet the Lord promised He would provide them with a child. And did they have a son then?

Ahhhh, nope.

Not even a girl was conceived. Did they have their son the next year, or the year after, or the year after? Nope. Not till he was 99 and Sarah 90—that's 24 YEARS later. Then they were this weird old couple having a baby.

Anyhow, Hagar was stuck in the middle of these two old people trying to conceive. Genesis 16:1, 2 says, "Now Sarai, Abram's wife, had borne him no children. She had a female Egyptian servant whose name was Hagar. And Sarai said to Abram, 'Behold now, the Lord has prevented me from bearing children. Go in to my servant; it may be that I shall obtain children by her.' And Abram listened to the voice of Sarai."

Hagar was a slave of Sarai (who became Sarah) and was used by her to have a baby. She conceived and then she got mad at her mistress. They fought each other with words. Abram said Sarai could do whatever she wanted with this human being. Hagar's treated harshly by Sarai. She's a slave. She's from Egypt. She's away from her home, culture, and family. Carrying a child in her belly, Hagar ran away.

She left her present "home" and fled to the wilderness. Then the LORD met her, or rather an angel of the Lord that I think is Jesus preincarnate. Think about how unusual this is. She's just some pregnant girl, some runaway. She hasn't been brought up in church. She doesn't know Jesus as her Savior. She hasn't memorized Bible verses. She hasn't done anything good or bad for the church. There isn't even a church building at this point. She just runs away and God meets her where she's at.

He asks her a question that chills my bones. He asks her where she came from and where she is going. She replies that she is fleeing. Then, in Genesis 16:9, "The angel of the Lord said to her, 'Return to your mistress and submit to her.'" Wait, what? Go back? And submit? But the Lord doesn't leave her there. In verse 11, He continues saying that He would multiply her offspring so that they can't even be numbered.

"And the angel of the Lord said to her, "Behold, you are pregnant and shall bear a son. You shall call his name Ishmael, because the Lord has listened to your affliction."

The Lord had listened to her cry. The Lord had listened to her and watched her flee. He had seen everything—all her fears, all her anxieties, all her misunderstandings, all her troubles, all her "what if's," all her mistakes, all her pain, and all her affliction.

"So she called the name of the Lord who spoke to her, 'You are a God of seeing,' for she said, 'Truly here I have seen him who looks after me'" (Genesis 16:13). *El Roi*—The Lord who sees. The Lord looked after her. The Lord cared. He saw her in her suffering. He recognized her agony and promised to take care of her.

God saw Hagar. God sees you and me. Again, I don't know your suffering tale, but God knows and He sees you. He sees you when you sit. He sees you when you stand (Psalm 139:1-3). He sees you when you cry (Psalm 56:8). He sees you when you laugh. He sees when you are suffering. He sees when people mistreat you. He sees when someone speaks wrongly of you. He sees you when you think you are all alone and therefore lonely. He sees you when you are lost. He sees you when you are forgotten by people. He sees you.

God comforts me as *El Roi* for He sees me, knows me, hears me, watches me, embraces me, and loves me. He sees you, knows you, hears you, watches you, embraces you, and loves you too.

February 8, 2021

Lord, please forgive me for acting proud and falling into one of the many temptations yesterday. I'm a sinner and I hate that I sinned against You. I have all of these anxieties and I know You said I can cast all of them to You. All? That's a lot. Ok…

"What if's" keep going through my mind. What if David doesn't pay me enough alimony? What if it's just in installments? What if I don't have the money to buy a house? What if I move into an apartment again? Will I be ok with that? What if it takes too long and I'm not out of Iris's house in August? What if Alex has to go back to his old school again? What if the bullies are back again and Alex gets beaten up? What if I can't be there for him? What if?

But what if it all happened the way it's supposed to happen? The way I want it to happen? Am I being selfish? Am I being oppressed by my abusive husband and thinking it'll never work out for my good? Is this the devil talking? Or my flesh? Or David?

Thank You for giving me the counselor to help me process all of this. Please use her to speak truth into my life. Please help us, Lord.

God's girl,
Molly

February 12 & 13 2021

Dear Jesus, thank You for this day of rest. Thank You Lord for giving me the inheritance money from my Great Uncle's passing. Thank You that You provided when I have nothing left to offer. I'm weary, Lord. So tired. Please renew my strength and replenish my body. I need Your strength emotionally, mentally, spiritually, physically, and psychologically. Please, I need You to hold me because I have no strength of my own.

Thank You for my counselor's words. Man, I've been run down since then. Thank You that I have Great Uncle's money and David can't get it. Thank You for getting rid of that fear that I have. Please rid me of all the fears from David.

Here I am, Lord, tired and broken. I have a lot of worries and fears. It's six months till August when potentially I would be moving to Dallas. David moved the date back to May for our mediation so he's withholding paying me till then. Basically, I don't know, and I want to know, Lord. I want to be in charge of my own money, and all David owes me. I want to buy a house with a big settlement from David. But Lord, are You're asking me to trust You? Do I have to let this go? It's silly to ask that question because I already know the *answer. *Sigh.* Ok Lord, here it is. I surrender to You everything—my money is Your money. My anxiety, my strength, my planning, and my past/present/future are all Yours. Here I am, broken and tired. Please be my strength today.*

God's girl,
Molly

February 14, 2021

Dear Jesus, I'm not satisfied with You and I know I should be. I'm sad about David and that he no longer is my Valentine. I want a new Valentine, but I know this is not Your time. I'm anxious about money, even though You just gave me money. I want to give a lot away, but I also want to save it all for buying a house. I'll tithe 10%, and the rest is in savings. What would You have me do with the money You gave me?

Lord, it says in the Bible to rejoice in You, but I have a lot of anxieties that prevent joy. I'm anxious about money, since I am now in charge of it. I really want to move into a house in Dallas that's mine.

David has so many "things" that I do not have. I think he should pay me what's fair. In April, it'll be eleven years since we've been married. He bought so much for himself and for other people, and I got the bare minimum. He's lied and cheated on me so many times. He committed adultery again and again, but I can't prove it. Would You help me prove it? So that I can get my fair share for the time we were married?

I dream of a house in Dallas where I welcome all people. A house that I own and can rent to a girl. A house where children who have been abused can stay and call their home. A house where foster kids can live. A house where the church can meet for city group once a week. A home where broken people, like me, can feel welcomed and safe. A home where Alex can invite friends over and have lots of sleepovers. A home where love covers everyone and that's Your love.

I want a place that is safe from the mental abuse that I went through, and the psychological and emotional abuse too. I want a house that is Your place that I can decorate and buy affordable furniture for at the thrift store like tables and chairs. A place where the decor and the lamps don't matter but where You are. I want a place where Your grace, mercy, compassion, forgiveness, kindness, and love are felt, believed, and embraced. I ask for that home. In Jesus' name, amen.

God's girl,
Molly

Chapter 18

Embracing God's Justice

I wrote this poem when I was just a little kid, but the words still hold true today.

Surrender

LORD, I'm holding on so tight,
Trying to get by on my own,
But it's not working out how I want it to,
Which causes all these tears and moans.

I'm frustrated at myself
For I know what I should do.
Yet no matter how hard I try,
I can't keep my focus on you.

My thoughts and actions wander,
My intentions are all about me,
My heart is not satisfied,
The way You designed it to be.

Father, You do love me so much,
You're faithful; I know You're always here,
And You do know best,
For everything in my life, every day and year.

You've asked me to give it all to You,
All my concerns, regrets, and pain.
Surrender is what You want of me,
To live for You should be my aim.

So God, here it is,
Everything. I'm giving it all to You.
I can't get through on my own.
Please take my heart and make it new.
-MG November '04

Galatians 5:13, 16 NIV
For you were called to freedom, brothers. Only do not use your freedom as an opportunity for the flesh, but through love serve one another…But I say, walk by the Spirit, and you will not gratify the desires of the flesh.

Psalm 116:1, 2 NIV
I love the LORD, because he has heard my voice and my pleas for mercy. Because he has inclined his ear to me, therefore I will call on him as long as I live.

❧ ☙

February 26, 2021

Thank You, Jesus, for being victorious over my life. Thank You for helping me realize that You are God and I'm not. You helped me process everything with my counselor. You helped me surrender over to You today again, and over the past 26 years. You helped me pay for my session by sending me $125 yesterday through checks that I got in the mail. You helped me grieve my broken marriage, let go of David and be ok with ending it.

You helped me remember that I tried to seek counseling, seek help to preserve our marriage but David refused. He sinned by committing adultery, telling so many lies and manipulations. He ran away from You, Jesus, and I realize now that I did everything possible to help him have a relationship with You.

He said no and he's done with our marriage. I let go and You caught me. I wish he had confessed and repented, but he didn't. I have no control over that. One day he might repent, but now he's living in sin and not repenting.

I still love David so much—unconditionally, I love him. Our marriage is over and I'm "moving on," but it's a long process. Thank You, Father, for helping me realize that You are in control. I am not. You are, and I'm so thankful You are.

It's a little silly, but thank You for my fall after counseling.

Iris paid for me to get tea and write but I fell out of the coffee shop, tripped, flipped over the stairs, landed on my head by the tables, and scraped up my knee. Thankfully, my tea flew out of my hand and the glass shattered away from me.

Three people came running and found me. One of the ladies "just happened" to be in nursing school and got me cleaned up. The lady who owned the coffee shop was so worried about me and ended up refilling my tea, telling me not to worry about breaking her cup.

I felt so silly because I knew there was a step but I forgot it was there, which is why I tripped. *Anyhow, I thank You, that I got to share my story about how great You are. I didn't tell the people all about You, just that You healed me and brought me through it all.* It was a reminder that I need to work on my book. She asked if I was going tell my story in a book. I said yes, I'm working on it.

When I rested at home, I happened to catch the movie *Togo.* It is a remake of Disney's 1995 animated movie called *Balto.* I loved that movie as a child. Both movies tell the dramatic story of the 1925 diphtheria outbreak in Nome, Alaska. The only serum was 500 miles away on a route that presented enormous hazards. One sled team raced the serum to the halfway point and one team raced from Nome to meet it half way. Togo and Balto led the two sled-dog teams featured in the story.

Togo is a true story of how God intervened in a disaster, like the children dying, and turned it into good, by the sled dogs mushing and carrying the medicine hundreds of miles. God allowed the people to find each other in the storms and snow to get medicine for the children. The same God who today allowed me to fall but not break my bones or cut myself on broken glass—the same God who allowed bad things to happen but worked them out for good.

God's girl,

Molly

March 24, 2021

How much of what I'm thinking and planning on saying to David at our mediation is justice or revenge? How much is undeserved favor from God and me trying to get what I deserve? How much is it me wanting to get from our marriage what he owes me? I don't know what David does with his money, but it's gone.

David owes me half of everything… What do I do? Do I simply ask for half? I read about suffering and God's comfort in 2 Corinthians 1 and the worry of David not paying me goes away. I no longer depend on his financial help. I depend on God and what He can do. This house, the one I'm potentially buying, is not about David's money. It's about God's money. He owns everything in the world and if He so chooses to give me a house, then so be it. If He chooses to provide for me through David, then so be it. I am God's girl, surrendering my life to Him in times of suffering and times of peace. It's funny that right now I have peace in suffering. Why? Because Jesus is good. Because the Spirit of truth is the same Spirit who strengthens me.

Oh Lord, here it all is—all my worries, fears, my powerlessness over David's emotions and money. I give all my anxieties over to You. I surrender everything to You. Thank You that You are God, and I am not. Thank You that You see everything—past, present, and future. You know exactly where and when and precisely how much my next paycheck is going to be.

Thank You for providing more than enough for Alex and me. Thank You for Iris and Larry who listened to You and opened their doors for us to live with them. Thank You that I cannot repay them in this life—but that You can. Please bless them and help them pay their next bills with an abundance. Thank You that they are Your people. Thank You that I am Your daughter. Thank You that Jesus has me surrounded by His grace. As He said to Paul in 2 Corinthians 12:9, 10 TPT, He is saying to me too:

> "His grace is sufficient and His power finds its full expression through your weakness." So, I will celebrate my weaknesses, for when I am weak, I sense more deeply the mighty power of Christ living in me. So, I'm not defeated by my weakness, but delighted! For when I feel my weakness and endure mistreatment—when I'm surrounded with troubles on every side and face persecution because of my love for Christ—I am made yet stronger. For my weakness becomes a portal to God's power.

Oh Jesus, I need You. Lord, would You help me buy a house? Would You be my Husband and help everything run smoothly? Would You be my everything? Would You be my strength?

I look at my life and someone else's life who does not know Jesus as intimately as I do—single Mamas have it so hard! I have lived from David's paycheck to paycheck. I have not known where the money was and even is coming from. I have lived without a husband for a while.

But God is bigger than my lack of a husband. He is bigger than child support. He is bigger than any accusation, feeling thrown away, belittled, neglected, divorced, being left for other women, and feeling like leftover trash. God says I'm His daughter—adopted by Him, redeemed by Him, saved by Him, looked after by Him, adorned by Him, cared for by Him, noticed by Him, enjoyed by Him, and loved by Him.

Just about every night I say something to my son. I say, "I love you so much, but you know what?" "What?" Alex answers. And then I reply with all honesty and sincerity, "Jesus loves you way more than I do." I say this to him because I want him to know that Jesus does love him way more than I do, and I love my son to the moon and back. I care for, look after, help, correct, discipline, adore, and absolutely love my son.

But sometimes I get frustrated with him. Sometimes I lose my temper. Sometimes I selfishly want my way, and he wants his way. Sometimes I just have him play games and watch movies all day. Sometimes, I do not love him enough.

But you know what? Jesus does. Jesus is always patient with him. Jesus always cares for him. Jesus always looks out for him. Jesus always opens His arms for Alex to get a huge hug. Jesus always knows what is best for my son. Jesus always does what is best for my son. Jesus is what is best for my son. Jesus loves my son way more than I do.

Yesterday went really well for my church plant. Pastor Brad preached on Ephesians 1:1, 2. He mentioned that an older gentleman said that we often portray ourselves as either the victim or the hero when we tell people how we came to the Lord. He also asked us what if we share the immense love of Christ?

I don't want to portray myself as the victim of David or the hero of my story. I don't want to say that I'm the victim of my stroke/heart surgery nor that I overcame all the darkness and "saved" myself. God is the hero. Jesus saved me and loves me sooo much that He died on the cross and rose from the dead so that I would be saved. His love is immeasurable. I'm so thankful for His love. That is how I want to be known—as the girl who Jesus loved.

The Lord warned me about David committing adultery years before we were even married. I remember reading Francine Rivers' book, *And the Shofar Blew,* and I heard the Holy Spirit whisper that David would commit adultery against me countless times. We weren't even dating at the time. I think I was 16 or 17 years old. I asked God if He wanted me to marry David even though he would one day commit adultery against me, and He said yes. Like the woman in Rivers' story, I was to be kind, compassionate, and loving towards David. Was I always? No way.

When David and Sandy were having the affair, I was so angry with them. I heard them and I knocked on the door, demanding that David come out and they stop. David, of course, denied that they were having an affair and used some lame excuse. He twisted the situation into him crying over my Alzheimer's and watching porn to satisfy him. I knew he was lying and Sandy was in the other room, quickly getting dressed. I saw her leave through the other door.

I knew he had committed adultery against me. But I didn't have proof, only my word against his word. I knew he had committed adultery against me with various women over the years. Unlike the couple who eventually reconciled and repented in the book, David wouldn't. I tried again and again to keep our marriage stable. But David drifted further and further away from Jesus and away from me.

Now our marriage is broken and I'm seeking a divorce. I'm being asked by Jesus to surrender even this broken marriage over to Him. I trust that He is in control, but I don't always.

God's girl,

Molly

Emails to my prayer partners

May 3, 2021

Hello prayer partners,

Today is the big day! Mediation starts in hours. Thank you all for praying for me and sending me encouraging messages. I was afraid of David and fearful of him. The Lord wisely directed me to not be afraid of David and to be brave. I looked up "fear" in the concordance of my Bible and He spoke to me through two passages in particular:

- 2 Timothy 1:7, which reads, "for God gave us a spirit not of fear but of power and love and self-control," and

- 1 Peter 3:14-17, which reads, "But even if you should suffer for righteousness' sake, you will be blessed. Have no fear of them, nor be troubled, but in your hearts honor Christ the Lord as holy, always being prepared to make a defense to anyone who asks you for a reason for the hope that is in you; yet do it with gentleness and respect, having a good conscience, so that, when you are slandered, those who revile your good behavior in Christ may be put to shame. For it is better to suffer for doing good, if that should be God's will, than for doing evil."

Pray that I will continue to not fear David and justice will be served. Pray that the Holy Spirit gives me power, love, and self-control. Pray that I will be ok to suffer for righteousness' sake while continuing to do what is right. Pray that I will honor the Lord in everything I say and don't say.

Pray that I would be prepared to give a defense for Jesus with gentleness and respect. Pray for my mind to be alert and ready. Pray for Jesus to win all the battles fought between David and me that I don't even realize are happening. Pray for wisdom, peace, grace, and mercy. Pray for me to be ready to fight battles by putting on the armor of God. Pray for David to no longer hide his money. Pray for David to have a soft heart and be willing to adjust.

Mediation is today from 9am-5pm. It's going to be a long day.

God's girl,

Molly

Later that day

Hello prayer partners,

Thank you all for your prayers today!

The Lord prepared me for not getting a lot of money this morning reading through 1 Peter 3:8-22. David has "no money" that we could see—he has no stock/cryptocurrency. Nothing.

I did get a lot, considering.

- I get benefit money from David's life insurance till Alex turns 18, if David dies.
- I get my birthday & Christmas EVERY year (from December 18th-28th).
- I get everything I wanted from our house.
- I get child support till Alex graduates and alimony monthly for 3 years.
- I get his work stock or payment if he switches jobs.
- I get to keep my bank account and my car (which I explained that my Church family gave me).
- He has to pay his debt.
- He keeps his bank account and car.
- He gets Alex one extra day twice a month on Wednesdays (2 days a month).

- He gets Alex on December 28th-school starts.
- We trade off Thanksgiving/Spring break/other holidays.

Thank you all for praying. My divorce will be finalized after we sign the papers in like a week or two.

God's girl,

Molly

May 5, 2021

Dear Prayer partners,

Thank you for your numerous emails. I must confess I feel like my cry for justice has not been heard. I read Psalm 32, telling God that David has been dishonest and manipulative. I feel as if all his lying schemes have prevailed. Yet, the Lord has shown me that there was no injustice in mediation, that He did favor me and not David in the mediation. He reminded me that He has provided for me time and time again. I ask that He will provide and that you join me in praying for that.

Pray for justice to be served around the globe. Pray for people to understand His justice. Pray for everyone to understand one day God will right the wrongs done to me and so many other people. One day. It may be in heaven. It may be on earth. But our Father God is the judge, He is righteous, He is holy, and He is just. He loves me so much. And He loves you so much. Praise Him for His love. Praise Him for His grace and mercy. Praise Him for His kindness.

God's girl,

Molly

May 6, 2021

Dear prayer people,

Thank you for praying for me. The Lord comforted me a lot and showed me how He worked justice in His way. My cousin helped me see how many other single moms do not get alimony/child support. She pointed out that I did receive justice for having primary care of Alex, making decisions about his school, and health issues.

That is justice because I was not allowed to even touch Alex last year when I lived under David's control and he had Alex under the control of his girlfriends. I can now decide what I think is best for

Alex, which is better for him since I seek the Lord for guidance and they do not love Jesus.

Iris also pointed out that I have the support of all of you and for that I'm thankful. I am thankful for all of you praying and offering me encouraging words.

- Praise: God is showing me justice.
- Praise: The Lord works everything out for His glory, not mine.
- Praise: I got health insurance for a low price.
- Praise: I've decided I'm going to rent an apartment.

God's girl,
Molly

☙ ❧

I want God to avenge me. Romans 12:19a says, "Beloved, never avenge yourself…" Can't I call on Hulk from the Avengers to come and smack David around? Right now that sounds great. Yet the remaining verse says, "...but leave it to the wrath of God, for it is written, 'Vengeance is mine, I will repay,' says the Lord."

God is bigger than Hulk. So do I expect Him to avenge me? I long for repayment. I have a set amount of money that I think is justifiable considering what he put me through. If David put me through all of that, I somehow felt justified if he paid me x amount. Yet, in Scriptures that's not how this works.

Joseph went through a lot in the Old Testament. He was sold by his brothers to be a slave in Egypt (Genesis 37:12-28). Constantly, his boss's wife allured him to sleep with her. He resisted time and time again.

Then one time he fled to resist temptation. She manipulated the scenario, pretending to be the victim in a sex scandal and pointed at him as the "would be" rapist. Joseph was falsely accused and falsely went to jail for years. Not days. Years. Once again, he succeeded at everything he did even inside a prison cell because "the Lord made it succeed" (Gen. 39:23).

God blessed him as he was in jail, as he was wrongly in jail. In time, he correctly interpreted Pharaoh's dream and got his reward—being second in charge of Egypt. The Lord helped him rise to power.

Out of desperation, his brothers came to Egypt to buy food because there was a famine where they lived. The same brothers who had sold him as a slave. Joseph could have sought justice. He could have sought revenge. He wisely tested them, trying to figure out if they still hated him or if they had changed their jealous ways.

Eventually, Joseph forgave his brothers. Forgiveness is hard. The Lord helped me let go of David and forgive him. I didn't just forgive him once and everything in my life was happy. No, I daily, sometimes hourly, had to forgive him. I was called by God to once again surrender to Him everything that had been done to me. I was to let go of all the wretched sin that had been committed against me.

I was to forgive not only David, but also the women with whom he had committed adultery. I did. Not once, not three times, but over and over and over again. There are days when I'm mad at them and forgiveness is really hard. Yet Jesus also forgave me. It says in 1 John 1:9, 10, "If we confess our sins, He is faithful and just to forgive us our sins and to cleanse us from all unrighteousness. If we say we have not sinned, we make him a liar, and His word is not in us."

Maybe there is sin in your life that you need to confess to Jesus. Maybe you need to forgive someone. Maybe you need to ask someone to forgive you. Maybe you lie, cheat, steal, drink, have sex and you're not married (or you're not married to that person). Maybe you gossip, you're prideful, maybe you get angry at your kids, frustrated at work, or you have road rage. Maybe the Spirit prompted you to talk to someone and you didn't. That's a sin of omission. Confess that sin to Jesus and be forgiven. Turn from that sin. Be redeemed by Jesus.

One day, David will be held accountable for his sins. David lied, manipulated, committed adultery, and abused me. Yet, the sin he did, not only affected me, but he sinned against God. The person who wronged you will one day stand before God and have to answer for their sins. We all sin. We will all be rightly judged by the Judge of everything.

All people, including David, will be held accountable for their actions. Ecclesiastes 12:14 says, "For God will bring every deed into judgment, with every secret thing, whether good or evil."

Back to Joseph's story, years later Jacob died and his brothers worried that Joseph would take revenge on them now that their father was gone. But in Genesis 50:19, 20, Joseph explains to them the ultimate reason why he went to Egypt.

> **But Joseph said to them, "Do not fear, for am I in the place of God? As for you, you meant evil against me, but God meant it for good, to bring it about that many people should be kept alive, as they are today."**

Joseph's brothers really meant selling him as a slave to be a bad thing, and it was. So often in our own lives, bad stuff just happens. Sometimes you can try your hardest and still you're in a horrible circumstance. Somehow, God can use your horrible past or present for your good. Most Christians have heard the verse, Romans 8:28: "And we know that for those who love God all things work together for good, for those who are called according to his purpose."

When I had the stroke at 20, I cannot even count how many people quoted that verse to me. How can this circumstance be "good?" I clearly loved Christ, but I had a stroke. I wanted to scream when I was pregnant with Alex because I could not "see" how my horrible pregnancy was good. Twelve years later, I'm thankful for Alex even though my pregnancy was hard. I can tell you now that God used my stroke for my good and is still using it to create good in me.

God is sovereign, and yet we don't always want Him to be. It would be so nice if He made everything good happen and we can be healthy, wealthy, and happy. Yet God created Joseph to have all these bad things happen, worked it out for his good, and the good of all the Israelites. The Israelites were saved from famine and they multiplied into a great nation while in Egypt.

On the flip side, we see that God doesn't always work everything out for good on earth. Throughout Scripture, there have been people killed, tortured, beaten, stoned, and wrongly thrown in prison. The prophet Jeremiah was beaten and thrown in jail (Jeremiah 20:2; 37:15). Stephen was stoned to death (Acts 7:58). James was killed with the sword (Acts 12:2). Paul had numerous near-death experiences (2 Corinthians 11:23-28) and eventually he was martyred too.

Hebrews 11 lists people of faith who God used in a mighty way. Then verse 35-38 says, "Women received back their dead by resurrection. Some were tortured, refusing to accept release, so that they might rise again to a better life. Others suffered mocking and flogging, and even chains and imprisonment. They were stoned, they were sawn in two, they were killed with the sword. They went about in skins of sheep and goats, destitute, afflicted, mistreated—of whom the world was not worthy—wandering about in deserts and mountains, and in dens and caves of the earth."

Sometimes our life choices or other people's life choices end badly on this side of earth. Yes, if you are a true Christian you get to live in heaven after death. But what about now? What if you're suffering and you just want it to end? Is there hope for you in this season of hardship?

There are days in my life that I consider bad. I pout, complaining that my life is unfair. I could go on about yesterday and how I complained to God about my life. Why is my life so hard? Why can't my life be like your average person's life? *Why, Jesus, why?*

I find hope if I keep reading Hebrews 12:1-3:

> Therefore, since we are surrounded by so great a cloud of witnesses, let us also lay aside every weight, and sin which clings so closely, and let us run with endurance the race that is set before us, looking to Jesus, the founder and perfecter of our faith, who for the joy that was set before him endured the cross, despising the shame, and is seated at the right hand of the throne of God. Consider him who endured from sinners such hostility against himself, so that you may not grow weary or fainthearted.

These verses show me, after the emotional abuse that David put me through, I can let go of everything and cling to Jesus. I know I've recorded this verse before but I want to dissect it with you right now. The first verse begins **"Since we are surrounded by so great a cloud of witnesses,"** referencing the previous chapters of people who had faith in God back in Hebrews 11. I would like to remind you that includes the people with the awful circumstances—and yet they too had faith in God.

"...Let us also lay aside every weight, and sin which clings so closely, and let us run with endurance the race that is set before us..." Let go of our burdens, release them to God. Not one time, but every day and every moment of every day.

Then the verse continues, urging us to **see our sin and repent**. Repent one time and everything is good in your life now? No, that means continuing to lay aside every sin, that means stop sinning and ask Jesus to forgive you for sinning. That means doing a 180, turning around from your sin. Sometimes there are sins in my own life that I constantly have to surrender over to the Lord and I think that's what's referred to in the phrase **"...clings so closely...."**

"...And let us run with endurance the race that is set before us...." We need endurance because life is hard. We are alive and run—not a physical race—but one metaphorically. I could not "run" while I was in the hospital with paralyzed leg/arm/mouth. Running is metaphorical. "Run" may mean to resist sleep or not to lie down and only binge watch TV. It may mean not to procrastinate. The race is living your life with perseverance so that you will run it well.

Endurance is hard. Endurance is pushing through, lasting a long time, persevering through your trial. Wouldn't it be nice if I could live life without endurance? Just sit back, relax and enjoy life? Well, Scripture tells us that we have to endure through circumstances that are difficult.

The second verse changes everything. It explains how we will find motivation to endure those hardships of ours: **"Looking to Jesus...."** I oftentimes did focus on Jesus in my hardships, but sometimes I also put my suffering first. Jesus is so vital, not only to Christianity but also to life's hardships.

To focus all your attention and expectations on Jesus is a lot. I expect a great deal from myself. Yet it says that Jesus gave us this incredible faith.

In this verse, why did Jesus die on the cross willingly? Because He knew you would be His. Can you imagine He "endured the cross" because He would one day choose you? He would one day forgive you and show you grace upon grace? Not because you did something good, but because He is good. Rising to life, He conquered death and its humiliation.

CHAPTER 19

Fear Man or God?

I'm afraid of many things. Fear of man, afraid of David and what he will do. The Israelites feared too and they suffered greatly in Egypt. Exodus 3:7 says, "Then the LORD said, 'I have surely seen the affliction of my people who are in Egypt and have heard their cry because of their taskmasters. I know their sufferings.'" The Israelites were fickle people, seeming to bend every time they were afraid and lacked faith. What if you were them? What if you lived in a time when the Holy Spirit didn't live in you? What if you were also afraid and lacked faith?

March 26, 2021

Dear Jesus, thank You that You do not lie to me. Thank You for always telling me the truth, Thank You that Your Word is true.

I've been going over my previous writing and realizing how much of what I wrote was based on lies that David told me and I believed. I went through years of psychological abuse and mistreatment. I thought I was going crazy and couldn't trust myself. I thought I was losing my mind because of Alzheimer's and that I was dying. I thought I was a tiny person who got everything wrong, and David was a patient man for still being married to me.

I thought that he was right and I was wrong. I thought that he was righteous and I was unrighteous. I thought that he had all the money in the world and I could not spend a penny unless he said so. I thought that I was impatient and he was patient. I thought that I was unlovable and yet he loved me. I thought that I was horrible, selfish, unkind, and he was good, selfless, and kind. I thought that I was faithless and he was faithful. I thought that I was impure and he was pure. I thought that I was untrustworthy and he was trusted.

But the Lord showed me how wrong that assessment was.

David lied about so many things for so long.

True thoughts because of Jesus:

- **I am loved by Jesus and nothing I do can take away His love.** Romans 8:38, 39

  For I am sure that neither death nor life, nor angels nor rulers, nor things present nor things to come, nor powers, nor height nor depth, nor anything else in all creation, will be able to separate us from the love of God in Christ Jesus our Lord.

- **I am a sinner but I am forgiven because I ask Jesus to forgive me.** Isaiah 1:18

  "Come now, let us reason together," says the Lord: "though your sins are like scarlet, they shall be as white as snow; though they are red like crimson, they shall become like wool."

- **I am not condemned because of Jesus.** Romans 8:1

  There is therefore now no condemnation for those who are in Christ Jesus.

- **I am chosen because He chose me.** Ephesians 1:4a

  …even as He chose us in Him before the foundation of the world…

I thought that I was not beautiful. I thought that I could never marry again. I thought that no man would ever love me. I thought that my story was too complicated, too much for someone else to bear. I thought I was poor, broken and little.

I cried in the car because Jesus made me complete. It's hard but I'm so thankful that I am free. Some people are not free from mistreatment, abuse, and lies told to them by others. Galatians 5:16-18 puts it this way. "But I say, walk by the Spirit, and you will not gratify the desires of the flesh. For the desires of the flesh are against the Spirit, and the desires of the Spirit are against the flesh, for these are opposed to each other, to keep you from doing the things you want to do. But if you are led by the Spirit, you are not under the law."

Thank You Jesus for helping me! Thank You that I can do all things, including live in 2021, through You. You are strong enough, all powerful, mighty, and my strong tower. Thank You for being my refuge, my safe haven, my strength and my lover.

I lift up this day to You. Thank You that Alex got to swim this morning with my dad at the hotel. Thank You that both my parents came and we got to eat out last night. Thank You that we're having a Minecraft birthday party for Alex this afternoon. Thank You that I was able to buy everything for his party because of the stimulus check.

Thank You for being God who is in control over everything. Thank You for giving me a choice to choose You. Lord, I'm holding on to You so tightly now that I've let go of David. You have given me such peace and reassurance that You are my Husband. I haven't taken anxiety/depression pills for two weeks now and honestly, I feel so free. I can trust and depend on You. All the money that David makes doesn't matter. I choose You over money. I choose You. Lord, thank You for Your reassurance for me to write a book. Thank You.

God's girl,
Molly

March 30, 2021

God whispered to me to trust Him and not apply for jobs right now. I'm going to wait till Alex graduates in May and then I'll apply. He has led me to write my book and showed me more of what it means to surrender in suffering. I'm not even going to drive for Instacart, which is scary!

He has provided for me so much. Before, I had nothing when I first left David's house. Through various friends and even people I don't know, He has provided me with enough to pay the bills. I am also going to stay single. I pray for the strength and self-control to be open for whatever God has today. I pray that I would not fear the unknown, lay my fears down at His feet, let go of all my anxieties, fear not my oppressors but fear God.

God's girl,
Molly

March 31, 2021

Mom M's birthday was yesterday. I miss her a lot. "Pour out all your worries and stress upon Him and leave them there, for He always tenderly cares for you" 1 Peter 5:7 TPT.

Ever since I was little, life stressed me out. I'm prone to be anxious. *Help me, Lord, to pour everything out to You—including my missing Mom M.*

God's Girl,

Molly

April 2, 2021

I was treated unjustly by David and his girlfriends for almost three years. First Peter 2:19 comforts me. "For this is a gracious thing, when, mindful of God, one endures sorrows while suffering unjustly."

Lord, thank You that I have found Your favor even when David was treating me unjustly. You have provided so much after I asked You to provide. You have given me Your peace regarding living on my own. You are good. Thank You! Thank You for Your love, which is steadfast, enduring, everlasting, and pure.

I'm human and I don't want to be treated poorly. I want justice against David now that I'm out of that situation. For whatever reason, David paying me half of what we own is what I think is fair. But is it? Can I be bold and tell him exactly what half looks like? I know that I allowed bitterness to overtake me in my thoughts. Forgive me, Lord? Take away my sin and help me to please You.

I take to heart the question Peter asks in 1 Peter 2:20, 21. "For what credit is it if, when you sin and are beaten for it, you endure? But if when you do good and suffer for it you endure, this is a gracious thing in the sight of God. For to this you have been called, because Christ also suffered for you, leaving you an example, so that you might follow in his steps."

Yes Lord, help me to follow after You. Help me to take all of the mistreatment and give it over to You, Here it is—all the wrong that David and his girlfriends did against me, all the anger, hostility, verbal abuse, injustices, belittling, and mistreatment.

Thank You that You do not treat me unjustly. Thank You that You are God who was and is and is to come. Thank You, Jesus, for Your faithfulness. Thank You for remaining by my side even as I endured mistreatment. Thank You that You are holy, true, righteous, King, shepherd, friend, and lover. Thank You for the following verses in 1 Peter 2:22, 23:

"He committed no sin, neither was deceit found in his mouth. When he was reviled, he did not revile in return; when he suffered, he did not threaten, but continued entrusting himself to him who judges justly."

Oh thank You! You are perfect and never lie. Thank You that You were verbally abused and yet, You did not return Your mistreatment with insults. I would have insulted the people who insulted me, but You did not. Thank You that I can learn from Your example. Thank You that You were not bitter, spiteful, or angry with the people. I get that way when I'm treated unfairly.

Thank You Jesus for dying on the cross so many years ago. Thank You for my brothers and sisters who were with me at the Good Friday service at our church. I cried tears of joy and blew my nose so many times. Thank You. Thank You that You are good despite my season of suffering.

Thank You for all the people who came early to pray. Thank You Lord for the two women who bravely had the courage to ask for prayer. Thank You for suffering physically, emotionally, spiritually and psychologically.

Thank You Jesus.

Thank You Holy Spirit for interceding for all of us, for praying, working, moving, and enabling us to be Your people. Thank You that You spoke and You worked in people's hearts. Thank You that You did that—not us.

Thank You that I'm free from the bondage, so to speak, that David was holding me in. Thank You that You set me free from the physical ailment of Alzheimer's, if I ever had it. You healed me of it. I don't know if it was real or fake and inflicted by David. Thank You that You set me free from him. Thank You that I am out.

Lord, so many women and men are not out and are trapped still. I pray that You will get them out of bondage. Help the abusive, manipulative, afflicting people to stop, repent, and worship You. Help them to realize that they are sinning against You and please forgive them.

Help the abused, manipulated, afflicted, and suffering worship You too. Get them out, keep them sane, rescue, and restore them. Please help those who need help. Help the Church see those who need help and help them. Be gentle with them, and may Your people be gentle with them. In Jesus' name, amen.

God's girl,
Molly

April 12, 2021

> …fear not, for I am with you; be not dismayed for I am your God; I will strengthen you, I will help you, I will uphold you with my righteous right hand. For I, the Lord your God, hold your right hand; it is I who say to you, "Fear not, I am the One who helps you."
>
> *Isaiah 41:10, 13*

Thank You Jesus for giving me courage to talk to my grandpa, saying that You make me happy, not my soon to be ex-husband. Thank You for giving me courage to talk to my family about the church plant.

God's girl,
Molly

May 7, 2021

Dear Jesus, I don't want to move yet again: 18 moves in my life, 11 in Alex's. This will be the 12th move for Alex. I really wanted a house so that he wouldn't have to move again and we could find a permanent place in Dallas. Lord, I know that You are in control of everything. I know that You saw me moving lots of times before it happened. I know that one day I'll have a home in heaven that won't change.

Lord, I left David and our house full of stuff. You say in Your word in Matthew 19:29, "And everyone who has left houses or brothers or sisters or father or mother or children or lands, for my name's sake, will receive a hundredfold and will inherit eternal life." *Father God, I love you, but David and his girlfriends did not like you at all, even hated You. It was so toxic in that house. I rejoice that I'm free from David's bondage.*

Yet, this is still another season of hardship moving into an apartment. You say in Your Word in Luke 14:27, "Whoever does not bear his own cross and come after me cannot be my disciple." *Is this another part of my "cross"—moving lots of times? Not having a home? Being a single mom?*

Living a life of poverty? Having hard circumstances? Having the stroke/heart surgery? Not being able to say the right words when I'm tired? Being weak from my stroke? Being so tired all the time? Having my right arm turning inward and hurting constantly? Is everything I've gone through, all the suffering, been for Your glory or my own? Has all the pain and heartache been about You or for me?

Is this a sin issue or merely a weight that I need to let go of? Do I have to endure and persevere and hope and have faith and love? Are my eyes fixed on You or are they distracted by the things of this world? Are they distracted by what I want to have, such as a permanent location? Or do they consider You? Help me look at You. Help me to cast off everything. Help me surrender. Help me to have more faith.

Help me to remember the cross and that You endured the cross for me. Help me remember that You despised the shame of the cross because I sinned. Help me remember that You overthrew death and rose from the grave. Help me remember that You endured hostilities against Yourself for me. Help me remember that and not grow weary or fainthearted. Help me remember that You are good. Help me, Jesus. Here I am, I'm Yours. In Your name, Jesus, amen.

God's girl,
Molly

May 9, 2021

Dear Jesus, thank You for showing me that Abraham had to move a lot too. Just look at Hebrews 11:8-10. "By faith Abraham obeyed when he was called to go out to a place that he was to receive as an inheritance. And he went out, not knowing where he was going. By faith he went to live in the land of promise, as in a foreign land, living in tents with Isaac and Jacob, heirs with him of the same promise. For he was looking forward to the city that has foundations, whose designer and builder is God."

Thank You Jesus, for Your love. Thank You that both Abraham and I have a city to look forward to, a permanent Home in Heaven. You didn't tell Abraham exactly where he was going at every hour, every minute. You waited. Then You showed Abraham where to go. Thank You.

Thank You for the allegory You have given me of living in tents. Tents are not permanent but they are used for just a mere moment. Sometimes they stayed a week, sometimes a month, and sometimes a year. But they always kept moving. Like me. In Jesus' name, amen.

God's girl,
Molly

May 11, 2021

I will not receive all that I'm promised until I die and go to heaven—eternal life, righteousness, justice, and perfection. Hebrews 11:39 says this so well. "And all these, though commended through their faith, did not receive what was promised." Just like these heroes of faith, I too have not received what I'm promised yet.

God's girl,
Molly

May 25, 2021

In my mind I know that You will provide, I know that You are faithful. But do I believe it in my heart? Do I trust You to provide? It's scary to be living in my own place. Thank You for working out my apartment and June 12th my move in date. You have clearly led me to be more involved in my church plant. You have shown me the neighborhood as I've prayed and prayed over what I am to do, where to live, who I am to be around, when I am to move, and why I am moving. You've led me to this apartment, to the people who live nearby, to Christians who rest in Your goodness, to the same school for Alex, and to this family of believers.

I "know" all these facts, and yet I'm still afraid. Afraid of David not paying alimony. Afraid that I won't get a job and will only have child support. Afraid that I will be alone and have guys take advantage of me. Afraid of my new possible job being too exhausting. Like every conscientious mother, I have been haunted by many nightmare scenarios about Alex and his future.

Yet all of this is outside my control. The future is outside of my control. You're asking me to trust You. Trust You when I'm afraid, worried, and struggling to make ends meet. Trust You to provide. Please provide. You have led me to this exact moment in time and I'm letting go of everything. Surrendering to You. Here it all is, my Lord. Everything past, present, and future. You know my past, David's past, Alex's past. You know everything. You know precisely what/where/why/how everything will work out. You are sovereign over everything and yet You allow us to choose. Thank You. And You know the future. You know when every knee will bow in reverence to You.

You know Alex's story too. I pray that I will know how to be there for Alex. Help him to blossom and bloom into a man after Your own heart. Help me to become a woman after Your own heart too. Help me today to serve You. Help me to ask for help from my new church about moving. Help me to do the job interviews well and know what to say. I pray that You would provide money for me. I pray that You will help David save and not spend all his money so that he can pay me. I pray that You will work everything out for Your good and glory. Help me be along for the ride, knowing that You are driving and not me. Help me to trust You. Help me to love You with all my heart, mind, soul, and strength. In Jesus' name, amen.

God's girl,
Molly

May 26, 2021

Lord, I'm so tired and weary. Please give me favor with a job. Please provide. Thank You for helping the apartment work out. Thank You for me signing the lease yesterday. Lately, I've been reading about Moses and his calling. There are many parallels to the Israelites and me.

God's girl,
Molly

May 27, 2021

Dear Jesus, I don't know what to do. Or rather I think You're leading me in a certain way and I'm kicking and screaming I don't want to go that way. I don't know what to do about jobs or working anywhere part-time. I don't think I can work even part-time because I'm sooo tired all of the time, and when I'm awake I can't always communicate. You've already given me so much money.

Amy suggested I work at Instacart when I can, spend the time I have with Alex, get used to living on my own, and try again with job hunting in the fall. I think that's the way You're leading me because all the jobs keep turning me down. I have money, it's not a lot. I had wanted to save that and buy a house, but that's definitely not in the picture right now. Lifting 30/40 pounds is not something I can do, and I'm going to have to tell the grocery store that I can't take the job. I am thankful I have a job, though I'm really wanting to work elsewhere and have a more permanent location.

I really want to work but Alex is a concern. Lord, will You provide? Am I having to trust You to work everything out? Am I not trusting You right now? What am I afraid of? I haven't trusted in money to keep me safe. No amount of money will ever satisfy me but only You can satisfy my soul. I know that You are my rich provider. I have money saved already, so I don't need a job. Alex is still too young to stay at home and it's not like I have help anymore. I know that I have the church, but I don't know anyone well enough to leave Alex with them.

I did it, I'm no longer looking for work. Ehh! It's scary. Lord, help me to trust You. Help me to do Instacart well. Help me to be with Alex well. Help me to meet and interact with the church well. Help me to pay all of my bills on time. Help me to be cautious with how I spend my money. Help me to use Your wisdom, Lord. Help me to rest well tonight and get up in the morning and drive for Instacart. Help me make the money I need. Help me to find everything quickly. Help me to carry the weight and not strain my back. Help my legs to walk, my mind to work, and my hands to carry the bags. In Your name, Jesus, amen.

God's girl,
Molly

May 28 & 29, 2021

Moses' fear and faith are evident in Exodus and Hebrews. In Hebrews 11:23-28, we see that Moses was very faithful, yet, he was also afraid. In Exodus 2:14, "Moses was afraid" when his deed of saving the Israelites was uncovered. He fled from Egypt because of fear that Pharaoh would end his life. After 40 years, he met God and "he was afraid to look at God" (Exodus 3:6). The LORD then presented to Moses that He's going to save the Israelites and use Moses. In Exodus 3:11, 12a, we read, "But Moses said to God, 'Who am I that I should go to Pharaoh and bring the children of Israel out of Egypt?' [God] said, "But I will be with you."

But Moses wasn't so certain that the Lord would be faithful and everything would turn out great. Oh no. His conversation with God was not over yet. He gave God one excuse after another and begged God to send someone else.

Why did God choose Moses? Why does He choose any of us? Is it because we are great, and can do it all for Him? Is it just that He's needing us to fulfill His desires? Is it because we are human beings who can work hard and get it all done? Or is He just a being in the air, "chilaxing" as my son says (chilling + relaxing), and doesn't even care about us?

The LORD does not give us in Scripture written detail about everything that will happen in our lives. I wish He did. But He does provide us with examples of how messed up life is. The Bible doesn't contain people who lived lives of perfection and got a lot of money doing life. No, it's made up of misfits just like Moses. He wasn't perfect. He stuttered. He messed up. He got angry and sinned. But God is perfect. God doesn't stutter. He doesn't mess up. When He gets angry, He does not sin.

I spent time meditating on the story of Moses and it encouraged me that God was able to use Moses to do the great task of delivering God's people even if Moses became afraid sometimes. And the encouragement God gave Him encourages me during these scary days when my tasks seem overwhelming.

I fear that David won't pay me. I fear that he won't pay the child support. I fear that if the money doesn't come through, they will kick us out of our apartment. I fear that I won't ever be able to work because of the stroke and its continuing effects on my body. I fear that Social Security won't accept my appeal and I won't get disability. I fear that COVID will take someone away from me, someone I love and cherish. I fear a lot of things.

I too have begged God to send someone else to encourage people. I too have brought up my mouth as an excuse. My mouth is not working the way it was designed to work. I can't talk when I'm tired, which happens a lot because I had the stroke. I just want to be a normal Christian who gets paid at work.

Yet, here I am writing to the world instead. So why has God sent me to you? To encourage and instruct you? Why can't He just choose someone else? I've asked God many times why.

These past few weeks have taught me that I can't do everything. Getting a job didn't work out. I applied for numerous jobs and I'm not qualified because I had a stroke and it has debilitating effects on me. Even with Instacart, I apparently brought the food to the wrong place. I was so tired yesterday that I guess I didn't pay attention. I thought I did, I got all of the items they asked for, and I thought I had brought it to their location. I guess I didn't. I'm still going to do Instacart one time a week, but I'm also going to rely on Jesus to make life happen.

I try to spend what I have the best way I can but the bills keep coming. I had hoped a job would fulfill me and provide what we need. Yet, fulfillment doesn't come through having a job. I know that mentally, but I didn't truly believe that. I really wanted a job and really wanted to work. Yet, the stroke happened. The heart surgery happened. And I guess the Lord is saying No.

It's scary because I don't have anything set in stone that God will provide for me. Yet, in the past He has provided for me so much. Since I first had my stroke God provided through thousands of people hearing about me. Strangers, friends, and family paid for everything from the time I laid unconscious in the hospital bed to now as I'm writing. I pray that He will also provide for Alex and me as we move into our new apartment.

God's girl,

Molly

In these fearful times, my imagination can run wild with both daydreaming and catastrophizing. I imagine finding a great husband who loves Jesus and loves me. I imagine that he will have a job to pay for all my bills. I imagine that he will want to have children and I can reverse the procedure I had to block my tubes. Wishing for more children, I could have children again, maybe even adopting. I imagine that I can serve and love others well enough. I imagine that is how God will provide for me.

Yet, on the reverse side, I imagine things going way wrong. Every fear rises in those imaginings and all God's promises are forgotten. The story of Moses and the Israelites greatly encourages me in my imagination. Could God have chosen me to endure suffering for a reason?

What if He chose me to write this story to help many come to know, love, and trust Jesus? What if He chose me to go through all this suffering and, not knowing why, so that you can read it? What if God chose me to endure the mental, emotional, spiritual abuse of my ex-husband to comfort some of you who are experiencing the same thing? What if God chose me to experience the unfaithfulness of my ex-husband to show you the faithfulness of God?

What if?

❧ ❧

After I separated from David, I had quite a few nightmares with David as the bad guy and me as the victim. I would wake up from the dreams, still shaken with fear. I fear man a lot, particularly David. I have to preach the gospel to myself to counteract the fear of David.

When talking to my new pastor, Brad quoted 2 Timothy 1:7 to me in reference to David. "God has not given us a spirit of fear, but of power, and of love, and of a sound mind" (NKJV).

God has not given me this fear that so often enslaves me. God is not the author of fear—He does not write my story so that I'm afraid. What does He give us instead? Power. Love. A sound mind. Not a crazy mind. Not a detached mind. Not a self-obsessing mind. Not a mind set on compulsion. Not a fearful mind. Most other translations put "self-control" instead of "a sound mind." And I think that both words refer to what Paul was telling Timothy—that God gives us a self-controlled and a sound mind.

David does not believe I have a sound mind. He still believes and tells people that I have Alzheimer's and am crazy. He tells them that I cannot take care of myself or Alex. He says I need him to survive. I may think David is delusional and living in fear, but he doesn't.

I've known him for 23 years and he fears a lot, but not God. He fears that I'm going to die. He fears that Alex won't have enough provision. He fears that he has no control over my life. He fears that Alex won't think of him as a "good" dad. He fears that people do not view him as mighty and powerful, on the one hand, but also the victim in his own story. He fears the world is going to end due to climate damage. He may laugh loudly and pretend that everything is fine, but I know the real David. And that David fears a great many things, except God.

Throughout the Bible, we are commanded to fear the Lord alone and not circumstances or people or anything else. The Lord shows us and tells us why throughout Scripture. In Proverbs 1:7 we learn that "The fear of the Lord is the beginning of knowledge; fools despise wisdom and instruction."

I struggle with fully understanding what the fear of the Lord is precisely. I am not wise and am still learning to fear the Lord. I do know what true devotion to God looks like for my life – utter surrender to Him who knows me. Obedience to His Word and complete reverence of Him.

Hebrews 10:23 in the Passion Translation gives me a reason to fear God. "So now wrap your heart tightly around the hope that lives within us, knowing that God always keeps his promises!" God always keeps His promises. David didn't. He would say he was writing me a birthday card, since words of affirmation are my love language, but he didn't. I think he gave me a total of two or three presents on all my birthdays and Christmases, and we were married for 11 years. He would come up with some excuse for missing them and I gave him mercy.

David broke a lot of his promises, beyond not giving me presents. I think that is why this verse is so important to me because God ALWAYS keeps His promises.

In His Word He promised to…

- Always tell the truth (Psalm 119:160).
- Always be there for me and with me as my strength and help (Isaiah 41:10).
- Be my shepherd (Psalm 23:1 and John 10:14).
- Always be my refuge and strength (Psalm 46:1).
- Always be faithful, loving, and merciful (Lamentations 3:22, 23).

That's why I can fear Him, worship Him, enjoy Him, and live in awe of Him.

Am I fearing God now? I'd like to say yes, but this is something that I'm still learning. How about you? Do you fear God or do you fear man?

Now that I am living on my own with Alex, I notice that courage grows in the times of fear. I live with both fear and courage every day. My fears coexist with the courage to affirm that God is enough for me, that I'm ok, that I can explore this new area with confidence in who God created me to be.

Every day He is faithful to me. And every day He reminds me to let go, surrender, and trust Him. It's scary to trust Him. It's scary to surrender. But as time goes by, faith turns into the courage to act with wisdom.

❧ ❧

Two Helpful Suggestions

Maybe you particularly fear *your* man or woman. Maybe you too have been married or are with someone who acts one way in front of other people, but is different at home with you. Maybe you too are in an emotionally, mentally, physically, and/or psychologically abusive relationship.

I don't have all the answers, but I know there is help. I pray the Lord uses this book to comfort you and bring you peace. I pray the Lord will deliver you out of your own abusive relationship.

Two resources can start you on your way.

1. You can call this number if you think you're being abused:

    Domestic Abuse Hotline
    1800-799-SAFE (7233)

2. Another helpful resource is **Called to Peace Ministries**, (www.calledtopeace.org). On the Called to Peace website there is a test to help women determine if they are in abusive relationships.

Many people in an abusive relationship recognize it only too well. But one surprising characteristic of some abusive relationships is not knowing you're actually being abused. Manipulative control is very confusing and makes you think you're crazy. That was my situation and taking the quiz awakened me to the true extent of what I had endured.

Take the quiz to see for yourself:
https://www.calledtopeace.org/resources/warning-signs-quiz

❧ ❧

Chapter 20

Surrender in Suffering

Surrender in suffering.
Surrender in joy.
Surrender in laughter.
Surrender in tears of sadness.
Surrender in times of hardship.
Surrender in times of hope.
Surrender in the good times.
Surrender in the bad times.
Surrender in tears of joy.
Surrender in excitement.
Surrender in thinking.
Surrender in people pleasing.
Surrender in pleasing God.
Surrender in behavior.
Surrender in all seasons of life.
Surrender in all things.
-MGM '21

Jesus has taught me how to surrender through my own suffering. To do so is not easy. I was abused mentally, emotionally, spiritually, and psychologically. David never hit me, but he beat me down with his anger and words. To me, he is a bully. It's amazing how many women have been abused by their own "David."

Many women have confided in me that they too were abused. Maybe you are in an emotionally abusive situation. Maybe you are being hurt by the words spoken to you. Maybe you are mentally feeling like you "can't leave" him because he pays for everything.

Verbally, David said "I love you," but his actions were not of love. Someone may say they love you, but do they really? The disciples said they would follow Jesus anywhere. Peter, in particular, said he would follow Jesus to the end of the world. Yet, when the time came, he didn't. Jesus foretold Peter's denial. Jesus spoke the truth, and Peter later said he did not know Jesus, right when He was being beaten. He denied knowing Jesus three times. The rooster crowed and Peter became aware of his denial of Jesus.

I think we often focus on the physical aspect of Jesus' death so much that we forget to notice how He suffered emotionally, mentally, spiritually, and psychologically. Just like I denied that David abused me until I left. Jesus was not only beaten with rods; He was beaten with words too.

Emotionally, Jesus suffered, as described in Mark 14:33. "He took Peter, James and John along with him, and he began to be deeply distressed and troubled." According to the dictionary, sorrow is "a feeling of deep distress caused by loss, disappointment, or other misfortune suffered by oneself or others." Feelings are emotional. Jesus was filled with sorrow because of what was going to happen. Emotionally, He was preparing for what would happen at the cross.

Mark continues in verse 34. "'My soul is overwhelmed with sorrow to the point of death,' he said to them. 'Stay here and keep watch.'"

When I was three years old, my uncle nicknamed me "drama mama" as I cried because he was borrowing our lawnmower for a day. Unlike me, Jesus accurately understood the significance of the events unfolding that night. His dramatic words captured the exact truth. He *would* die that night. Mark 14:35, 36 says it this way. "Going a little farther, he fell to the ground and prayed that, if it were possible, the hour might pass from him. And He said, 'Abba, Father, all things are possible for You. Remove this cup from Me. Yet not what I will, but what you will.'"

Now that's surrender in suffering. Jesus said it and released everything over to God. He wanted what God wanted. "Yet not what I will, but what you will." Even in this time of anguish. This time of suffering.

His friends were not there with Him, emotionally, in His hour of suffering. Can you imagine Jesus in anguish, praying to God to ease His suffering? He woke up his three closest friends, not once, but three times in verse 37. Begged them to stay awake, pleading with them to just be with Him. "'Simon,' he said to Peter, 'are you asleep? Couldn't you keep watch for one hour?'"

He must have felt so lonely. He knew His hour of torture was coming soon. The tension and stress of that agony literally dropped blood from his forehead. I have been stressed out before, but never like that. That feeling in His heart overwhelmed His body to sweat drops of blood.

Lies were thrown at Him. Mark 14:56 refers to false witnesses at his trial. He was beaten with words. The anger of the mob tore Him down. Notice the anger increasing, louder and louder. Mark 14:63, 64 TPT puts it this way: "Then, as an act of outrage, the high priest tore his robe and shouted, 'No more witnesses are needed, for you've heard this grievous blasphemy.'

Turning to the council he said, 'Now, what is your verdict?' 'He's guilty and deserves the death penalty!' they all answered."

Note the exclamation point.

In Luke 23:18 in the Passion Translation, it says they erupt[ed] with anger. At times, David would enter the room with anger in his vocal cords and his whole body shaking because he was angry. I cringed emotionally as well as physically when that happened.

Jesus must have felt emotionally torn because the people were angry with him. The soldiers mocked Jesus, as we see in Mark 15:16-20. Verbally, Jesus was abused. I'm hesitant to say that He was "abused" because He is the Most High God, King of Kings, Righteous and Just. Yet, when I read the text that's what I see.

He, Jesus, was mocked, scorned, beaten, and ridiculed. Verbally and physically, people did not adore Him with love. No, they said evil things to Him that were NOT true. They rejected Him, physically, mentally, emotionally, and verbally. They said mean things to Him, and He did not scorn them. He did not throw it back in their face by saying they were lying. He did not yell at them. He did not tell them He was dying FOR THEM and for their sin. He was quiet, as a lamb about to be slaughtered.

All this Jesus suffered for me. He willingly went to the cross. I don't like reading or hearing or seeing about Jesus' death on the cross. Ever since I was a girl, I cried and cringed at the crucifixion. I now read the Bible, specifically Jesus' crucifixion, in utter thankfulness. I realize that should have been me—I should have died because I sinned against God. I deserve death, and yet Jesus took that upon Himself. Jesus bore my sins and your sins. First Peter 2:23-25 (NIV) expresses this so beautifully.

> When they hurled their insults at him, he did not retaliate; when he suffered, he made no threats. Instead, he entrusted himself to him who judges justly. He himself bore our sins in his body on the tree, so that we might die to sins and live for righteousness; by his wounds you have been healed. For you were like sheep going astray, but now you have returned to the Shepherd and Overseer of your souls.

Jesus did not die out of anger that you would sin. He did not die grumbling that you would mess up. He did not die wishing that you would do better. He did not die like a disapproving, disappointed Judge. He died out of love. He died so that you would be redeemed. He died so that you can be saved. He died so that He can forgive you. He died so that you can forgive other people too.

Matthew 16:24 says, "Then Jesus told His disciples, 'If anyone would come after me, let him deny himself and take up his cross and follow me.'" Sometimes we have to suffer like Jesus did on the cross. Sometimes we have to endure trials because Jesus had to endure His own trial. Sometimes that means we have to surrender over to Him our life and the lives of other people we love. Sometimes that means we have to surrender in suffering.

I will never know the full truth of what happened in my life due to the lies of my ex. I have to surrender that over to God because He knows the truth. He deserves all the glory and praise. I get the opportunity to surrender to Him in my own suffering.

A final encouragement

Sometimes when I look out at the clouds full of rain, the clouds cover the sky. With dark clouds blocking the sun, I cannot see the sun, but I know the sun is still there. When the darkest storm clouds fill my own world and the thunder rumbles all around me, I know the Son is still there. I know that God is faithful despite our worst circumstances.

Jesus is still the Light of the World. He is my hope, my joy, my love, and my everything.

I pray you will learn to surrender everything, every moment of your life to Him who suffered greatly for us. I pray for you to trust Jesus, and know He sees you in your own suffering. I hope that this book has brought you great comfort to know that you're not alone in your hard times.

The sufferings we endure are worthwhile in the long run, though the hardships seem like they go on for a long time. According to 1 Peter 5:10, 11, we can rest in His promise about our suffering:

> And after you have suffered a little while, the God of all grace, who has called you to his eternal glory in Christ, will himself restore, confirm, strengthen, and establish you. To him be the dominion forever and ever. Amen.

Epilog

I wrote this book, had various people proofread, and then edited, edited, edited. Meanwhile, I worked a part-time job at a hamburger shop. In May 2022, I started back to college online to get my Bachelors of Science in Religion: Christian Counseling. I graduate in March 2024 and then am pursuing certification with the Association of Biblical Counseling. Counseling people is what I dreamed about for years, and I'm really excited about pursuing this career. We will see what God does through this wonderful opportunity.

Also in May 2022, after I saved and saved, I bought a house. My Home is in heaven and I forever look forward to the day when I get to see Jesus face to face, but that time is not now. I'm excited to be a part of a community and open my home to many people at community group.

Following Jesus is scary at times. I have not always surrendered and let go. Even now, I'm anxious about the thousand things I have going on. I have triggers of my ex and the domestic abuse I went through living with him. Some days are great, and other days are not so good.

The Lord has told me repeatedly to trust Him. Surrender. Let go. Breathe. Stop clinging to everything. Let go. The Lord has brought me emotional healing from the trauma of my ex-husband. Peace, His calming peace, has entered my heart. Sometimes I'm anxious, but other times I go to the Lord in prayer and His peace soothes my heavy heart. I let go of all my worries and surrender to Him even in my suffering.

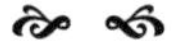

Acknowledgements

I want to thank everyone who helped me write my book!

Thank you, Briele Warren, for spending two years helping me comb through journals and editing my writing. I would not have written this book without your determined, generous help.

Thank you, Mom and Dad, for everything you endured when I was in the hospital. Thank you for your wisdom, love, compassion, grace, and mercy.

Thank you, Jane, for your kindness, love, and for being my sister.

Thank you, Iris and Larry, for your loving patience in rescuing us out of my ex's house and into your home.

Thank you, Alex, for being my silly, stubborn, loving son.

Thank you to my prayer team for praying for me and for this book. You received my email messages for years and faithfully prayed for me.

Thank you for all the people who prayed for me when I first had the stroke and heart surgery. The Lord heard every single prayer, He remembered, and answered.

Thank you, Nikki McGowen, Dallas Gossett, Hannah Barlett, Jane, my mom, and Julie Anderson, for proofreading my book and providing me with feedback.

And thank you, Dionne Carpenter, for helping me with editing, formatting and publishing. Thank you for your encouragement to keep writing, your dedication to Scripture, and your wise counsel as we worked on my book.

Afterword

From elementary school through high school, Molly was the kind of girl you looked up to. She was the 'mother' of the group, if you would, and would always ask you how you were doing, and if there was anything she could pray for. Although we were only a year apart, Molly exuded confidence and friendliness—traits that evaded me during our growing-up years.

I recall one time, our families were at the park (along with a number of other homeschooling families), and we older siblings were playing tag on the playground with all of our younger siblings and friends.

A nearby mother called the cops on our group, because from her point of view she saw a bunch of teenagers "terrorizing" the playground. I do not blame her, as unfortunately it has become increasingly unusual to see teenagers play with their younger siblings, but we posed no threat to the playground equipment nor our siblings.

When the local park ranger came up to the playground in response to the woman's call, he explained the situation. I was furious, embarrassed, and didn't trust myself to say a non-angry word. After all, we didn't do anything wrong. The rest of the group just looked at one another. But Molly stood in front of the group, nodded her head, and assured the officer that "Yes, we understand. Yes, we will be careful. Thank you, Sir."

That was the kind of young person Molly was. She took responsibility and cared for others with a peace and calm about her, and we respected her for it. She was always involved in her community, and throughout the years I never heard her pass a judgment or make an unkind remark. When she married David—another of our childhood friends—we rejoiced and prayed that her life would be blessed beyond measure.

Fast-forward ten years. I find myself editing a book, penned by our dear Molly, detailing her incredible and heart-wrenching story. I've cried and wrestled with my inner thoughts as I look back on how I've spent these last ten years of my own life. The hurdles that I've faced pale in comparison to the suffering that she has gone through, and yet, my heart has still been filled with ungratefulness, entitlement, bitterness, and lost faith.

Although I was raised in the church, as I entered adulthood, I became disillusioned with the materialistic, traditional, judgmental, selfish attitudes and actions I saw in the supposedly 'Christian' people around me. I allowed imperfect people to cloud my perspective of the life that the Christ of two thousand years ago actually lived.

Combing through Molly's personal journals and heartfelt prayers has been a wake-up call for me in two ways. First, it has been a stark reminder that I lack a thankful heart towards my Savior. And second, it has reaffirmed my faith in God and my place in this world. I still have more questions than answers. However, I know that I need to be intentional in my diligent searching of what it means to serve Jesus and others in love and selflessness.

Molly's internal wrestling reminds me of King David in the Bible, who reached out to God in every circumstance—good or bad, large or small—and God heard him. In the Psalms, we have chapter after chapter, verse after verse of David crying out to God—praising Him, begging Him for help and mercy, and thanking Him for His goodness. David struggled with horrible sins, yet God still called him a man after His own heart.

Similarly, we see Molly through her sorrows and joys, struggles and triumphs—as she strives to turn to Jesus every step of the way. And in the midst of her suffering and broken dreams, she clings to her Jesus, and reminds all of us to persevere through, trust in, and surrender to the One who holds the world in His hands.

Above all, surrender.

Thank you again Molly for this opportunity. I have been forever changed because of it.

Briele Warren.

Made in the USA
Coppell, TX
27 October 2023